Leading Through Language

Leading Through Language

Choosing Words That Influence and Inspire

Bart Egnal

WILEY

Published by John Wiley & Sons, Inc., Hoboken, New Jersey.
Published simultaneously in Canada.

For general information on our other products and services or for technical support, please contact our Customer Care Department within the United States at (800) 762-2974, outside the United States at (317) 572-3993 or fax (317) 572-4002.

Wiley publishes in a variety of print and electronic formats and by print-on-demand. Some material included with standard print versions of this book may not be included in e-books or in print-on-demand. If this book refers to media such as a CD or DVD that is not included in the version you purchased, you may download this material at http://booksupport.wiley.com. For more information about Wiley products, visit www.wiley.com.

Library of Congress Cataloging-in-Publication Data is available

ISBN 978-1-119-08771-7 (hbk)
ISBN 978-1-119-08773-1 (ebk)
ISBN 978-1-119-08775-5 (ebk)
ISBN 978-1-119-17660-2 (ebk)

Cover Design: Michael J. Freeland
Cover Image: © iStock.com / heibaihui

Printed in the United States of America

10 9 8 7 6 5 4 3 2 1

Dedicated to
my wife, Emily Mather, and my son, Kye Egnal,
whose words and love inspire me every day.

CONTENTS

PREFACE AND ACKNOWLEDGMENTS

In March of 2014 I received a cold call from a literary agent, Brian Wood, who wanted to talk to me about the possibility of writing a book. In a to-the-point style I have come to appreciate, Brian dispensed with pleasantries and said, "I'll get right to the point – I've read your writing about leadership communication online, and you should write a book."

I politely told Brian that while I was flattered, the timing wasn't good. After all, just three months ago my life had changed drastically: I had just assumed the CEO role of The Humphrey Group, I had relocated my family from Vancouver (where I had been running our Western Canadian operations for five years) back to Toronto, and we had just moved into a new house and were settling in. I hadn't even gotten my first 90 days in! But Brian was not to be deterred, and he suggested a quick chat when he was next in town. I accepted, and as our meeting drew closer, I mulled over the possibility of writing a book. I started to realize there were some compelling reasons to consider proceeding.

First was the ability to share our intellectual capital with a much broader audience. Having spent over a decade at The Humphrey Group, I had developed a greater passion for our unique leadership communications methodology; over and over clients told us that it demystified the critical skill of inspirational speaking. They loved the practicality and how it could be applied to virtually any interaction. And frequently they told us (because most were executives or senior leaders), "I wish I'd had this earlier in my career!" A book would allow us to provide our intellectual capital not just to those with an executive training budget or a company focused on leadership development; it would be accessible to anyone who had a few hours and a passion for communication.

Second, I knew a book would be a boon to our clients and the broader discourse of leadership communication because our Founder, Judith Humphrey (who is also my mother), had recently written *Speaking as a Leader: How To Lead Every Time You Speak*, and it had been very well received. Over and over clients told us it gave them an easily accessible look at the fundamentals of inspirational speaking. They bought and shared copies with their colleagues and direct reports. And it wasn't just clients who loved the book – we regularly had people all over the world write in and ask to work with us because of the book, or simply to share with us how it had made a difference for them. Building on the foundation Judith had laid with *Speaking as a Leader* was an exciting possibility.

Third, I was excited about writing a book because it could afford me the chance to continue "coaching" even as I took on the CEO role. While Judith's vision had been to create The Humphrey Group over 25 years ago, my vision was to grow the firm. With her support I had moved to Vancouver and spent five years hiring and building our team. Our business had expanded dramatically, from a company with an office in Toronto and a few employees to a global business with offices in Toronto, Vancouver, Calgary, and Mexico City and with nearly 50 people who today deliver training around the world. When I became owner and CEO in January 2014, I fulfilled a life-long dream to carry on Judith's legacy. Yet, in only three short months I was already realizing that the demands of the CEO role would increasingly take me away from individual coaching and training; writing a book was a way to reach out and continue to help others develop their ability to lead and inspire.

So, when Brian arrived in Toronto for our meeting, I had come around to the idea and was ready to proceed. In June of 2014 I retreated to my in-laws' cottage on Georgian Bay, about two hours north of Toronto, to prepare the book proposal. Away from Wi-Fi and even cell phone reception, this was to be the first of many productive writing retreats. Free from distractions (except my road bike, which I'd ride for a few hours each day to take a brain break), I penned the proposal that Brian then shopped to publishers, which, six months later, led to

Wiley offering me a contract to publish the book you are now holding in your hands.

Though my name goes on the front cover, *Leading Through Language* was really authored by so many individuals inside and outside of The Humphrey Group.

I owe a debt of thanks to Judith Humphrey, our Founder, for creating not only The Humphrey Group but also the intellectual capital that remains the foundation of the work we do today. She taught me how to think, write, and speak clearly, and to help others do the same. Her willingness to provide clear guidance and coaching to our clients served as a shining example to me as I built my own relationships with executives. And her own writing – *Speaking as a Leader* and now her new book *Taking the Stage* – was proof that I could produce a book of my own. I was fortunate to have her assistance when writing the chapter on rhetoric, an area where she brings deep expertise.

This book also draws on the collective wisdom, experience, and expertise of my colleagues at The Humphrey Group. For nearly 15 years it has been my great privilege to work with and learn from each of them. From the day I joined the firm, they have invested their time in teaching me about leadership communication, and I continue to learn from them to this day. Writing a book is tremendously time-consuming, and I would like to thank the members of my management team – Rob Borg-Olivier, Jessica Young, and Aram Arslanian – for their support and understanding when I couldn't be present because I had to meet another writing deadline. I'd like to thank the members of our administrative team who helped in innumerable ways: Melissa Wilson, who put in a huge amount of work on interview transcripts, research, and overall project management; Niamh Farrelly, who was the only member of our firm to read the proposal; Emily Hemlow and Margo Gouley, whose keen copy-editing eyes were invaluable in making sure there were no mistakes in the text; and Kaylee Saloranta, whose research on visionary leaders uncovered some fine examples I was able to incorporate at the eleventh hour.

Many people outside our firm made invaluable contributions as well. At the heart of this book are over 50 hours of interviews I conducted with executives, managers, doctors, lawyers, professional athletes, and thought leaders. Their collective willingness to spend their time and open their minds to me led to a rich set of examples – and to a deeper understanding of how leaders use language to inspire action in a wide variety of workplaces. You will read quotations, all used with permission, from many of those whom I interviewed.

I'd like to thank Emily Alonzo, Michael Barry, Les Dakens, Bruce Derraugh, Jorina Elbers, Chuck Fallon, Martha Fell, David Gibbons, Margo Gouley, Robert Gouley, Guy Jarvis, Dane Jensen, John King, Almis Ledas, Frederic Lesage, Toms Lokmanis, Geoff Lyster, Jeff Medzegian, Michael Morrow, Geri Prior, Steve Reid, Jay Rosenzweig, Serge Roussel, Anne Sado, Daniel Skarlicki, Phillip Smith, Bruno Sperduti, Marcella Szel, Anna Tudela, Susan Uchida, Greg Wells, and Darren Yaworsky for their time, wisdom, and belief in this book.

This book was made possible only because Brian Wood, my agent, read my writing and used the language of leadership (direct, confident, and authentic!) to inspire me to take on the project. It was also made possible because Karen Murphy at Wiley said "yes" to the proposal and believed the book should be written. Thanks to both of you for believing in me.

The team at Wiley has been a pleasure to work with. Thanks go to Judy Howarth, Tiffany Colon, and everyone else at Wiley who provided support through the whole project.

I also had a local editor, Beth McAuley, who got the manuscript into top shape before I sent it off to Wiley. Her excellent editing allowed me to focus on the writing process. Thanks for being a crucial second set of eyes.

This book would not have been written without my father, Marc Egnal, a gifted writer and accomplished historian. Through high school, university, and in my early career he taught me how to write with clarity and precision. His many years of advice and patient guidance served me well when it came time to write this book.

Finally, deepest thanks have to go to my wife, Emily Mather. Over the year that this book was written she endured countless writing retreats and even consented to being interviewed. But more importantly, she provided tremendous moral support and encouragement. My wife has always been someone whose positive, caring, supportive words have inspired me to excel. She is my sounding board, coach, and the love of my life.

Leading Through Language has been a pleasure to write. It has created a deeper and more nuanced set of beliefs about language, which will lead to more effective coaching and teaching at The Humphrey Group. It has also reconnected me with our intellectual capital in ways that renewed my love of our work. I hope you enjoy reading this book as much as I enjoyed writing it.

If this is your first experience with The Humphrey Group, I'd encourage you to connect with us so you can continue to build your leadership communication skills. We are online at www.thehumphreygroup.com. You can follow our firm on Twitter at @THG_Inc and you can follow me at @THG_Bart.

And now, *Leading Through Language* . . .

INTRODUCTION

After 15 years of coaching executives and managers on how to communicate as leaders, I have reached a simple conclusion: jargon in the business world is getting in the way of effective leadership. Now, I could tell you why I believe this, but instead let me share with you three stories that illustrate this reality.

STORY 1: "AM I BEING FIRED?"

My first story begins with a simple question posed to me two years ago by Jessica, a friend of mine who worked as a director of sales in a mid-size Canadian technology company: "Do you think I am being fired?"

She'd called me up for advice on a Friday afternoon because she had just had a very confusing conversation with her boss. She had been called into a meeting to discuss her group's performance, which she admitted was lagging due to the low performance of some of her sales reps. She had grown unhappy in the role and had been contemplating a move, but hadn't told anyone yet.

After 30 minutes of seemingly productive dialogue with her boss about how to make changes to her team to improve sales, she was feeling better. Then her boss said, "Well Jessica, we have to wrap up, and I'm glad we talked because we need to be aligned on our human capital strategy on a go-forward basis."

Jessica paused, unsure of what to say to this, or even what it meant.

Her boss continued, "Look, I know your personal blue-sky growth plan sees you growing with an organization that's a segment leader, and while we hope we'll get there, we're not sure when. I appreciate that, and as we rightsize our workforce, we're prepared to release you to the market to support you realizing your potential."

He then glanced at his watch, said he needed to run, and left the room without giving her a chance to respond. She sat in stunned silence, trying to decipher what she'd just been told. At which point she called me. Was she being fired with cause? Offered a severance package? Or simply being asked if she was planning to leave in the near future?

STORY 2: "WE WANT HER OFF OUR ACCOUNT TEAM"

My second story begins over coffee with Jeff, a senior partner at an international consulting firm. Jeff was based in Chicago but worked globally. I had gotten to know him when he and I were both hired by the same client and partnered to prepare an important board presentation. Now it was years later and we were catching up while Jeff was in Toronto to see another client. We were talking about talent development and Jeff was bemoaning the inability of his up-and-coming analysts and associates to instil confidence in clients when he brought them to meetings. I asked him to give me an example.

"Just last week, I brought Sandra, one of the brightest minds on my team, to a crucial meeting with Railway X. Railway X is an existing client with whom we are hoping to expand our work over the coming years. Sandra had already been doing great work for this client. She has an MBA from Stanford. She can build a financial model with her eyes closed. And she'd been doing the legwork for several months on the needs assessment for this client, and had built the model that was integral to our recommendations. In the presentation I wanted to make sure she was front and center because, if we won the engagement, she would be leading the delivery team and working closely with the client.

"After I set the stage, I asked Sandra to explain our findings. It was – pardon the pun – a train wreck. She started off by saying, 'Well,

I'm not sure why I'm here because this was a real team effort but I guess someone has to share the results. And I should qualify what I'm about to present by saying these are just our conclusions and we could be wrong. But we do think there is maybe an opportunity to strip $20M in costs out. Still, I'll defer to Jeff on this one because he's really the guy with deep expertise on the transportation sector.'

"The upshot of this," he continued, "was that they immediately lost all confidence in her and turned to me for the rest of the presentation. But I hadn't done the detailed work she had and so wasn't able to provide the substantive answers they needed. In the end, we didn't get the work, and they also told me they wanted Sandra off their account for our existing business because she seemed too junior."

STORY 3: "WHAT EXACTLY ARE YOU SAYING?"

Recently, I was invited by one of my clients, the CEO of a small but highly successful investment management firm, to sit in on his weekly leadership team meeting in Toronto. He asked me to take notes and then comment on the effectiveness of each presenter.

The meeting began with a young but senior asset management executive going on and on about how great their U.S. office in Boston was. He then paused for effect and summarized: "So, you see, it's essential that we leverage Boston on a go-forward basis if we are going to grow AUM."[1] The audience looked around at one another, at him, and then again at one another. After about 10 seconds of silence someone started clapping, convinced the matter was mercifully closed.

I knew I was supposed to sit quietly, but if no one else would ask, then I would. I put my hand up and said, "Excuse me, what exactly does it mean to leverage your Boston office?"

The speaker fixed me with a puzzled stare, and then silently appealed to his CEO for help. When the CEO looked back at him with a blank look, the young executive realized no help would be forthcoming. He turned back to me, and with a deflated tone replied, "Well, I don't exactly know, but there must be something good we can do with them."

THE RAMIFICATIONS OF JARGON

These three stories have one thing in common: the language being used was getting in the way of leadership.

In the first story, Jessica's boss was unable to tell her directly that he didn't think she had what it took to develop her team, and that he was going to offer her a severance package. He used baffling corporate-speak to avoid telling her the truth, and he hoped that he could get her instead to resign and "pursue other opportunities." Neither happened, and the result was three months of tension followed by a termination and litigation.

In the second story, Sandra's technical brilliance and expertise were undermined by her weak and self-deprecating language. The client could not see past her projected lack of confidence to the value she could deliver, and lost all confidence in her. Sandra's linguistic minimization was not only detrimental in this interaction, but, as Jeff told me, ultimately held her back from advancing to partner, where her skills and sharp mind would have easily been the equal of others.

In the third story, the young asset management executive was using jargon to mask the reality that he hadn't developed anything of substance to share with his colleagues. The result was that his audience was confused, could not understand what he was saying, and ultimately felt a lack of confidence in his ability to play a growing leadership role in the firm.

JARGON IS EVERYWHERE IN THE WORKPLACE

I wish I could say that these examples of linguistic ambiguity, self-minimization, and corporate jargon are isolated incidents, but they are anything but. In my 15-year career as a leadership communication coach, and now as the CEO of a firm whose sole purpose is to help our clients communicate as leaders, I am repeatedly confronted by individuals whose use of language confuses and alienates their audiences while undermining their ability to lead.

The Concise Oxford English Dictionary defines language in two distinct ways:

1. The method of human communication, either spoken or written, consisting of the use of words in a structured and conventional way.
2. The system of communication used by a particular community or country.

Implicit in these definitions is that language is used by people to communicate ideas in a way that is understood by the audience. It is the choice to use both a *structured* and *conventional* set of words that allows both speaker and audience to grasp the ideas being expressed. It is a common system, chosen by a *community* or *country* to communicate together.

Yet, as anyone who has worked in the corporate world (or in government or the not-for-profit sector) can tell you, language is seldom a path to clarity. Instead, if asked to define language, most tenured corporate workers might describe it as follows:

- A jargon-filled, often baffling set of words, some of which actually exist and others which are constructed to demonstrate superiority and knowledge at the expense of the audience.
- A collection of empty clichés and confusing buzzwords that distract the audience from the lack of clear thinking being expressed by the speaker.
- A hieroglyphic-like amalgamation of acronyms and technical terms that few can decipher without consulting a corporate anthropologist.

As I've seen words and expressions like "synergies," "leveraging," "net-net," "disintermediation," and "core competencies" start overtaking words that can actually be found in *The Concise Oxford* or in *Merriam–Webster's Dictionary*, I've asked myself a few questions. Namely:

- Why is this happening?
- What is the impact of using these words?

And, perhaps most importantly:

• What can be done about it?

The short answer to these questions is that jargon, buzzwords, and corporate-speak usually exist because of a dearth of clear, powerful thinking. The impact of this language is that audiences are left confused, alienated, and uninspired. The solution is to use the language of leadership.

What is the language of leadership? Simply put, it is language that clearly and powerfully brings your ideas to life for your audience.

I chose to write this book to show you why you need the language of leadership and to teach you how to leverage the tools you'll need to reach your stakeholders – or, in plain English, to use words that engage and inspire everyone you speak with or write to.

IF YOU WANT TO LEAD AT WORK, THIS BOOK IS FOR YOU

This book is written for anyone who wants to lead in the workplace.

If you are an executive who wants to inspire your organization to embrace your vision for the future and bring it to life, this book is for you. It will show you how to articulate that vision with words that energize your employees.

If you are a manager who aspires to help your team realize its potential, this book is for you. It will show you how to be purposeful when you speak to your team, and to use authentic, positive language that will enable you to reach and motivate your people.

If you are a technical expert who wants your ideas to be heard and acted upon, this book is for you. It will show you how to present your recommendations with language that is direct, passionate, and jargon-free. In short, this book is not just written for CEOs – it is written for anyone in the workplace who has ideas they believe in and wants those ideas to inspire others.

At The Humphrey Group, our mission is to help our clients lead every time they speak. We believe that leadership is not based on title or number of direct reports, but rather on a person's ability to inspire others to follow. We also believe that this ability to inspire is not innate but rather a skill that can be learned, developed, and mastered.

If you want to learn this skill, this book is written for you. It will show you how to consciously and deliberately define and communicate your ideas using jargon-free language that will engage and motivate others.

THE HUMPHREY GROUP

Leading Through Language: Choosing Words That Influence and Inspire is based on, and expands, the intellectual capital of The Humphrey Group.

Some quick background on my firm. The Humphrey Group was founded in Toronto by Judith Humphrey in 1988. The firm provided speech writing and delivery coaching to C-level executives who wanted to deliver inspiring formal talks. Over the next 25 years, two trends led to the evolution of the business. First, companies began viewing the ability to speak as a leader not as something reserved for the C-suite, but instead as a core competency at all levels of the organization. Second, with the rise of email, PowerPoint, and more recently social media, communication became progressively less formal.

The Humphrey Group evolved and grew in response to these trends. When Judith founded the firm, the bulk of our services were provided to the C-suite; today we work with all levels of organizations, from front-line specialists to project managers to vice presidents. In the early days of The Humphrey Group our work was primarily executive coaching; today we still provide one-on-one coaching, but the majority of our clients participate in seminars and other group-based training, which has exponentially expanded the number of people we can help. And when The Humphrey Group was founded, our intellectual capital focused on speeches – how to prepare and deliver them so they were inspirational. Today our methodology focuses on how to inspire in the everyday interactions – meetings, emails, phone calls, presentations – where our clients tell us the pressure is on for them to show leadership.

When I joined The Humphrey Group in 2001 out of university, I quickly developed a passion for our work. It was tremendously rewarding to coach clients so they could define and bring forward the ideas they were most passionate about. There was nothing more rewarding than hearing from a client who had secured a promotion, gained support for a major project, or increased the engagement level of her team. I quickly came to see that the work we did was transformative because it developed in our clients the skills they needed to lead others – long after their work with me and the firm was done. I began to see that there were thousands of individuals out in the world who could benefit from what we offered, but we would have to expand to serve them. With the support of Judith Humphrey, I set out to lead this expansion in 2007, moving to Vancouver, BC, and opening our second office. Over the next few years I oversaw the expansion of offices in Calgary, Alberta, and Mexico City. Our firm grew in size and we began working much more in the United States as well as globally in places as diverse as Japan, Abu Dhabi, England, India, France, and China.

In 2012 I was proud to become President and CEO of The Humphrey Group, completing a long-held dream. Our vision as a company is to continue to grow, to become the world's premier leadership communication firm. We want to be able to reach and help anyone who wants to lead when they speak. Today, with four offices and nearly 50 people working around the world, we are taking exciting steps toward making that vision a reality.

This book is part of that quest. It draws on the intellectual capital The Humphrey Group has developed over its 25-year history. It also expands on that intellectual capital by delving deeply into language and how leaders use it, something we normally can spend only a few hours on with our clients.

How This Book Is Structured

Leading Through Language: Choosing Words That Influence and Inspire has two main sections. Part I examines why jargon exists and discusses its implications for leaders. The six chapters in this section explain how leaders look at language as a tool they can use to influence and inspire others. They then look at the implications of using jargon and tech-speak for those who wish to lead. The chapters examine jargon on a spectrum, starting with how it can benefit leaders and culminating in how it undermines and damages them.

Part II presents a solution to those wishing to avoid the linguistic shortcomings described in Part I. It explains how to approach all communication as an act of leadership and then how to use language that can convey ideas with energy, clarity, and conviction.

The first two chapters in Part II provide an overview of what it means to communicate as a leader. Chapter 7 looks at how to adopt a leader's mindset. While there are many reasons to communicate (e.g., to impress, to share information, to gain understanding), leaders recognize that their primary imperative is to shape beliefs and inspire action. Leaders consciously and intentionally use every interaction to create believers and to move others with their thinking. This purposeful approach to communication enables leaders to never miss an opportunity, and Chapter 8 shows how leaders capitalize on these opportunities by "scripting" themselves. This term refers to how leaders organize their thinking around a clear message, and this chapter shows how to do so consistently.

The remaining chapters of the book – Chapters 9 through 20 – look at the ways in which leaders can choose words that reflect leadership. Chapter 9 provides an overview of what it means to use the language of leadership. Chapters 10 through 20 each look at one specific way to choose words that influence and inspire. For example, Chapter 10 talks about how to use language that is visionary ... Chapter 13 how to use authentic language ... Chapter 18 how to use language that is concise, and so on.

ABOUT THE EXAMPLES

Leading Through Language is brought to life through real examples of language in the workplace, so let me provide some context for the examples you will read. In addition to the authors I quote and the public-domain speeches I reference, the examples and stories in this book are drawn from two main sources.

First, many are drawn from the extensive interviews I conducted for this book. Over the course of six months I conducted over 50 hours of interviews. The majority of these interviews were with executives in large North American corporations, but I also interviewed doctors, athletes, academics, and teachers. My goal was to learn about language and leadership in a wide range of workplaces and professions. Each interview was recorded and transcribed, and each individual has signed off on my use of their comments in this book. In any instance where you see a directly attributed quotation, it was likely drawn from one of these interviews.

Second, I drew on my 15 years of work as an executive coach to share examples of what the language of leadership does and does not sound like. In particular, I share many stories and examples of clients whom I have coached to help them strengthen their leadership communication skills. Because confidentiality is important, I have changed all identifying details when I share such examples, including names, company names, industry, or anything else required to preserve anonymity. You will know I am protecting confidentiality when I refer to the individual only by their first name (like "Jessica" in the first story in this chapter). What I don't change are the examples of language – uses and misuses – that are relevant to this book.

SUMMARY

By the time you have completed reading *Leading Through Language*, you will be able to understand why so much language in the business world is ineffective, irritating, and detrimental to leadership. Yet, I'm also confident that you will come to see that language is not only a jargon-laden minefield to be crossed with great care but that it can also be a tremendously powerful tool for reaching and inspiring your audiences.

The time has come for this book to be written.

- No longer should we "solution for that bogey."
- No longer should we "unlock our people potential by optimizing our human capital rightshoring."
- No longer should we "pursue synergistic efficiencies through cross-functional operationalizing."

Instead, the time has come to replace this kind of jargon with clear, powerful, and inspiring language – the kind that moves listeners to act. In short, the time has come for all of us to use the language of leadership.

Notes

1. Assets under management, for those without an acronym dictionary.

Part I

THE MANY FACES OF JARGON

INTRODUCTION TO PART I: WHY DOES JARGON EXIST AND WHY SHOULD LEADERS CARE?

Anyone who wishes to lead – to inspire others to act – must approach communication with conscious intention. Anyone who wishes to lead must treat every interaction, from a town hall meeting to a conference call, as a chance to reach audiences and move them to act. And anyone who wishes to lead through communication must think consciously about language and, in particular, the language that many use as a default in the world of work – jargon.

Jargon has always fascinated me – yet it also puzzled me. When I embarked upon this project, I had many questions about jargon that I had been wrestling with for some years. Specifically:

- Why does jargon exist, particularly since most people loathe it?
- What are the benefits and consequences of using jargon?
- Should leaders use jargon and, if so, what kind?

Having spent over a decade teaching leadership communication skills to managers and executives, I had formed some strong opinions about how these questions should be answered. Specifically, I had developed a strong view that when it came to leaders, jargon was ineffective or even detrimental. Leaders would be better served avoiding jargon in favor of the kind of clear language and powerful rhetoric that can reach and inspire audiences.

My viewpoint has been developed over the course of many years of listening to thousands of our clients from a wide variety of industries complain about jargon. Invariably they have described it as confusing, unnecessary, lacking in substance, and frustrating for audiences. They expressed a desire to have it eliminated from their own speech as well as from their workplace cultures, and indicated it was only their need to fit in and speak in the language of their organization and industry that convinced them to use it.

INSPIRATIONAL LEADERS THROUGHOUT HISTORY HAVE SPURNED JARGON

My conviction was also reinforced whenever I examined the words of inspirational speakers in more recent history. Over and over, I was struck by the consistent absence of jargon in their language and the presence of powerful rhetorical devices like repetition, metaphor, parallel structure, and alliteration (more on these and other patterns of rhetoric in Chapter 20).

Consider Winston Churchill, who inspired Britain through the power of his words and voice during World War II. He used no jargon; instead, he used rhetoric to share his convictions. Here is an excerpt from his speech to the House of Commons on June 4, 1940, delivered shortly after the British had been driven out of Europe by the Germans:

> Even though large tracts of Europe and many old and famous States have fallen or may fall into the grip of the Gestapo and all the odious apparatus of Nazi rule, we shall not flag or fail. We shall go on to the

end. We shall fight in France, we shall fight on the seas and oceans, we shall fight with growing confidence and growing strength in the air, we shall defend our island, whatever the cost may be. We shall fight on the beaches, we shall fight on the landing grounds, we shall fight in the fields and in the streets, we shall fight in the hills; we shall never surrender....

Churchill's use of repetition and parallel structure (constructing sentences in the same way to aid in understanding and retention) helped him rally a nation in its darkest hour.

John F. Kennedy was also known for the power of his language – and, like Churchill, favored rhetoric over jargon. Here's the famous conclusion of his inaugural address on January 20, 1961:

In the long history of the world, only a few generations have been granted the role of defending freedom in its hour of maximum danger. I do not shrink from this responsibility – I welcome it. I do not believe that any of us would exchange places with any other people or any other generation. The energy, the faith, the devotion which we bring to this endeavor will light our country and all who serve it – and the glow from that fire can truly light the world.

And so, my fellow Americans: ask not what your country can do for you – ask what you can do for your country.

My fellow citizens of the world: ask not what America will do for you, but what together we can do for the freedom of man.

Finally, whether you are citizens of America or citizens of the world, ask of us the same high standards of strength and sacrifice which we ask of you.

Kennedy's use of antithesis in his "ask not what your country can do for you" sentence saw him contrast two sentences with different ideas. This powerful use of language made this one of the most memorable calls to action in modern history.

Churchill and Kennedy are but two examples. Margaret Thatcher, Martin Luther King Jr., Bill Clinton, Golda Meir, Nelson Mandela, Ghandi . . . the list of great leaders throughout history who chose not to use jargon but to use powerful and clear language to bring their ideas to life is a long one.

RESPECTED CORPORATE LEADERS ALSO SKIP THE JARGON

It isn't just world leaders who have used rhetoric and skipped the jargon. Today, many of the corporate world's most respected executives and thought leaders make the same choice when deciding what words to use. Here's Sheryl Sandberg, in her 2010 TED Talk "Why We Have Too Few Women Leaders," using conversational, personal language to describe her aspirations for women in leadership positions:

> My generation really, sadly, is not going to change the numbers at the top. They're just not moving. We are not going to get to where 50 percent of the population – in my generation, there will not be 50 percent of [women] at the top of any industry. But I'm hopeful that future generations can. I think a world that was run where half of our countries and half of our companies were run by women, would be a better world. And it's not just because people would know where the women's bathrooms are, even though that would be very helpful. I think it would be a better world.[1]

Sandberg's ability to use personal language and to convey an aspirational vision without jargon has inspired countless women (and men) and led her to write *Lean In: Women, Work and the Will to Lead*, an incredibly influential book that has reshaped the dialogue around women in the workforce.

And here's Steve Jobs, delivering a commencement speech in 2005 at Stanford University. Jobs had just been diagnosed with cancer. In his speech, Jobs explained that his diagnosis was shaping how he was living his life:

> When I was 17, I read a quote that went something like: "If you live each day as if it was your last, someday you'll most certainly be right." It made an impression on me, and since then, for the past 33 years, I have looked in the mirror every morning and asked myself: "If today were the last day of my life, would I want to do what I am about to do

today?" And whenever the answer has been "No" for too many days in a row, I know I need to change something.

Remembering that I'll be dead soon is the most important tool I've ever encountered to help me make the big choices in life. Because almost everything – all external expectations, all pride, all fear of embarrassment or failure – these things just fall away in the face of death, leaving only what is truly important. Remembering that you are going to die is the best way I know to avoid the trap of thinking you have something to lose. You are already naked. There is no reason not to follow your heart.

It's not just in speeches that Jobs used simple, clear language while creating a strong personal connection with his audience – his corporate remarks also made use of similar words to reach and inspire his listeners. Jobs's gift was to take the "tech" out of technology and use language that resonated with everyday people who had little interest in gigabytes or wireless frequencies.

Sandberg and Jobs are but two modern-day examples of corporate leaders whose language is jargon-free. From Jamie Dimon to Warren Buffett, from Jeff Bezos to Richard Branson, some of the most inspiring corporate leaders of today are using language that is clear, powerful, and easily understood.

BUT THERE ARE *SOME* BENEFITS TO JARGON...

We know that most people dislike and are irritated by jargon. Great leaders in history have passed on it. Modern-day thought leaders avoid it like the plague. So jargon must be something that leaders – and those who wish to lead – should avoid at all costs, right? Well, the answer is that jargon should *almost* always be avoided by those who wish to speak as leaders – but not always.

This conclusion was not one I arrived at immediately. It was one I formed over the course of more than 50 hours of interviews. During these interviews I was surprised to hear that almost no one I was interviewing automatically condemned its existence or use. Many argued that in some instances it was valuable. Consider some of the things I heard.

Guy Jarvis, Chief Commercial Officer at Enbridge, a Canadian pipeline company, told me that jargon allowed people from the same industry to speak more easily among themselves:

[Jargon] seems to pop up, in industry and business all the time, and I think that a lot of the time, the technical stuff gets used because it becomes easy for all. Generally speaking within an industry, people are going to know what you're talking about... [so the value of] technical jargon within an industry is just an ease of use.

This view was echoed by Susan Uchida, Vice President of Learning at the Royal Bank of Canada (RBC), Canada's largest company:

My personal belief is that jargon becomes your own sort of corporate language. It becomes a terminology that is acceptable. Everybody understands. So, particularly in a business like ours where you might pick up on management consulting words like leverage... that word dominates because, now, everybody understands what that means. It is almost [as easily understood as a word] like car.

Daniel Skarlicki, Edgar Kaiser Professor of Organizational Behaviour in the University of British Columbia's Sauder School of Business, echoed that jargon has an efficiency benefit:

Jargon begins as a form of efficiency.... It's a shorthand...it helps us be more efficient.

He also pointed out that jargon

...builds a social identity. [For] example, in my field [there is an academic journal] called *Journal of Applied Psychology*. Nobody ever says *Journal of Applied Psychology*, [they] just say JAP. So, when you use the word, I use the word. I understand the word and it helps kind of build our sense of understanding for each other.

Over and over in my interviews, the executives and professionals I spoke to emphasized that, when used carefully, jargon could serve the interests of leaders.

We can group these positive types of jargon into two categories:

- **"Shorthand" jargon.** This consists mainly of acronyms or short terms that may refer to larger concepts. (Think of a CEO talking about EPS – earnings per share – when speaking with analysts, or a finance leader talking about "closing the books" for a company's year-end.) Leaders know that as long as their entire audience understands what such shorthand refers to, the benefit is faster, quicker communication.

- **"Shared identity" jargon.** This is the kind of distinct jargon that every profession and industry has; using it and using it effectively can bring people together and create a sense of belonging. (Think about football, a sport in which extensive and unique language like "carrying it across the goal line" or "throwing a Hail Mary" binds teams together and whose use signals true fandom.) When used and understood in context, this level of jargon can create strong social ties and signify belonging.

Yet, even these benefits come with caveats: the jargon that allows for expediency can be detrimental to those who do not understand it but are assumed to. Jargon that creates a shared identity for some excludes others simultaneously.

THE MANY FACES – AND CONSEQUENCES – OF USING JARGON

During the interviews, for every positive comment I heard about jargon, I heard 10 negative ones. For every cautious concession that jargon created a shared identity, I heard a corresponding note of concern around the pitfalls of excluding others by creating such a shared identity.

That is why, despite these benefits, leaders should be cautious and deliberate about making the choice to use jargon. Part II of this book outlines what kind of language leaders *should* use, but in Part I we will look at the different types of jargon that exist, why jargon is used, and the effect this use has on others.

It is important for leaders to recognize that words we identify as "jargon" fall into many categories. Each category is a collection of terms that is used for different reasons and that influences the ability of leaders to convey their ideas effectively. In addition to the two "positive" types of jargon – shorthand and shared identity jargon – I found four broad types of "negative" jargon.

When I say "negative," I mean that while it may convey some benefits, it is ultimately detrimental to those who wish to lead through their communication. Each type is used for different reasons, and each type has a different effect on its users and those who hear it. These are the four categories:

- **"Assumption-driven" jargon.** This is the term I use to describe jargon that is a product of a speaker's inaccurate assumptions. (Think of speakers who use acronyms while under the mistaken impression that their audience knows what they mean, or who use technical terminology without taking the time to explain what that meaning is.) Leaders are mindful of such assumptions and the fact that they must avoid making them if they wish to reach their listeners.

- **"Inflation" jargon.** This is the term I use to describe jargon that replaces simple, clear language with more impressive-sounding words. (Think of someone who says "utilize" rather than "use.") While this jargon can make speakers sound more knowledgeable, leaders know this kind of language creates barriers between them and their listeners and should be avoided.

- **"Lack-of-clarity" jargon.** This term refers to jargon that is used to paper over a lack of precise, clear thinking with impressive-sounding words. (Think of the executive who touts a merger as "synergistic" without defining exactly what that means.) This jargon differs from assumption-driven jargon because, in this case, the speaker *actually*

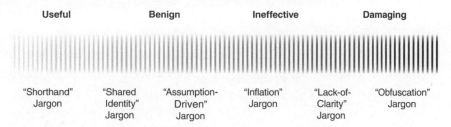

| Useful | Benign | Ineffective | Damaging |

"Shorthand" Jargon   "Shared Identity" Jargon   "Assumption-Driven" Jargon   "Inflation" Jargon   "Lack-of-Clarity" Jargon   "Obfuscation" Jargon

Figure I.1 The Jargon Spectrum.

doesn't have a clear sense of what the jargon means. Leaders know this kind of jargon is dangerous because it either baffles an audience or undermines speakers who are incapable of explaining it.

- **"Obfuscation" jargon.** This term refers to jargon that is designed to intentionally baffle and confuse an audience. (Think of the language used by companies to "sanitize" the difficult realities that accompany mass layoffs.) In some cases this kind of jargon is a well-intentioned attempt to avoid conflict, in others it can be a more diabolical effort to confuse and bewilder. Leaders know that being direct and honest is crucial and so avoid this kind of language at all costs.

Most jargon that people rebel against and are frustrated by fits into one of these four categories.

WHY JARGON EXISTS: THE SPECTRUM

After finding that there were two "positive" and four "negative" categories of jargon, I then plotted these categories on a spectrum, depicted in Figure I.1. This spectrum, which I will refer to as the Jargon Spectrum (ironically creating a new piece of jargon), is designed to allow you to evaluate what kind of jargon you are hearing or using, and what its implications are for leadership. The spectrum begins with jargon that is useful for leaders, progresses to jargon that has no positive or negative effect, moves to jargon that is ineffective for leaders, and culminates in jargon that is highly damaging.

The intention behind the Jargon Spectrum is to show that jargon is used for many different purposes, and that leaders should carefully consider its benefits and limitations as they seek to inspire others. I include this chart in each chapter, and will highlight the term being used so you can see where it fits on the spectrum.

SUMMARY

Jargon is not going away. It is found in every profession, company, and culture. It can help create community and save time, yet it can also create confusion and push audiences away. By understanding the many faces of jargon, what causes people to use it, and the benefits and consequences of its use, leaders will be better equipped to make careful choices about the language they use. The next six chapters look more closely at the six types of language plotted on the Jargon Spectrum and consider whether they help or hinder leaders who wish to inspire others.

NOTES

1. http://www.ted.com/talks/sheryl_sandberg_why_we_have_too_few_women_leaders/transcript?language=en.

1

YOU MUST START WITH LEADERSHIP

I t was the night before a critical company town hall and Rick, the
CEO of a struggling manufacturing company in New Jersey, was
wondering what to say to his employees. For many years, his company had been recognized as an efficient, tightly run business. They
had always been proud of manufacturing in the U.S., and of their
ability to turn a profit while doing so. They had also built incredibly
strong relationships with their customers. But over the last three years,
things had been going downhill for Rick's business. His competitors
outsourced production and were able to drive their costs down. Rick's
major customers valued their long-standing relationships and were at
first unwilling to switch to the now-lower-cost competitors. But over
time the gap between Rick's prices and his competitors widened, and
even long-standing, loyal customers began to defect.

To respond to these pressures, the leadership team – made up of
Rick, his Chief Operating Officer, his Chief Financial Officer, and
a few of his Vice Presidents – had begun a relentless "productivity
optimization drive" to "close the margin gap and improve the value
proposition." Yet, a full year into the "strategic initiative," Rick and his

leadership team were frustrated that their efforts were not bearing any fruit. They realized that the company's middle managers and front-line workers were not buying in to the plan. They knew this because these employees were increasingly vocal in their criticism of the strategy, which they saw as taking the company away from relationship-building and toward cost reductions. Around this time, a tenured manager confronted Rick on the manufacturing floor. Pointing a finger at Rick, he said, "I've been here 20 years. This company was built on relationships with customers – not trying to drive costs out. We need to stay focused on our relationships. They'll be there for us forever as long as we take care of them."

Rick's CFO had put together some slides that had numbers showing loss of market share, departure of key customers, and forecast of margin gaps, but Rick knew the slides wouldn't resonate with his employees. The night before the meeting, he went to sleep wondering what he was going to say.

The next morning Rick arrived at work and went to the cafeteria where the town hall meeting was being held. The company's 500 employees packed the room. Rick strode to the front of the room. He felt the tension and anxiety in the crowd. The slides prepared by his CFO were loaded into the projector. He began to speak.

"Good morning. I've got slides here but I'm not going to use them. Instead, I'd like to tell you a story. Growing up, my parents ran a small hardware store. Relationships with the community were everything, and my parents built their reputation on service. Then a big box store arrived and slowly my parents' business started to feel the pinch. It wasn't surprising – this giant store could sell many products for less than it cost my parents to purchase them wholesale. It was a hard lesson for my parents to learn – that relationships are only valuable when price is comparable. My story has a happy ending. Spurred by the arrival of this giant competitor, my parents forced themselves to change what they sold and strike better deals with their suppliers. They were able to reduce their prices to a level where the relationships they had mattered. Today, that big box store is still there – but my parents, who are in their 70s, have carved out a niche and still enjoy working to this day."

Rick paused.

"I know we all value our customers and are committed to serving them well. But, like my parents found out, it won't matter if we can't also continue offering our customers pricing that is competitive. Our customers value their strong relationships with us – but there will come a point where they will cross the street to our competitors despite those relationships. That's why we need to pull together now..."

As Rick spoke, he could see that his audience was paying attention and listening to what he was saying. He could see that his story was resonating with his employees. In the days that followed, the positive responses he received told him that his words had changed a lot of minds and had done what he wanted them to do: create the unity in the company that was required for change.

Why was Rick's talk effective? Because he was able to translate the technical knowledge he had (margin compression, market share, productivity gap, etc.) into clear, powerful language. Because he was able to take a dry business case and present it as a personal story that was meaningful to both him and his audience. Because he was able to show empathy for the employees in his audience and validate the legitimacy of their views while still challenging them to adopt new beliefs. In short, Rick was effective because he used the language of leadership.

Moments like the one Rick created don't happen by accident. They are the result of a deliberate choice to speak as a leader, of extensive preparation to ensure the message is clear, and of careful selection of words that will ensure that the message resonates with the audience.

Over the course of my career and in researching this book, I have come to firmly believe that language can be a tremendous tool for individuals who wish to influence and inspire others, just as Rick did that morning at his company's meeting. When speakers make the conscious choice to choose words that enable them to lead (and to avoid those that may undermine their ability to do the same), they are using the language of leadership, and the results are powerful.

WHAT IS LEADERSHIP?

Before we look at the ways we can use the language of leadership, we must first step back to discuss what it means to lead, and why the link between leadership and communication is so fundamental.

There is no one model for leadership. In your life and your career you have undoubtedly worked for or with people who you would describe as leaders. Some of them may have even been your manager (if you are lucky!), but many others are individuals whom you have wanted to follow.

Some leaders are big-picture thinkers, while others are detail-oriented. Some leaders are hands-off delegators, while others dive in and work side by side with you. Some leaders are big personality extroverts, while others have a quieter style that draws you in. In the example above, Rick was a personable, human leader. He sought to connect on a genuine, individual level with his employees to build understanding and unity.

Given these differences, it's important to define what is common among leaders. So here it is:

A leader is someone who inspires others to act.

That's it. Leaders are able to create believers who accept and act upon their ideas. They are able to do this not dictatorially but inspirationally. And they are able to achieve this regardless of their skills, level of education, or title, and regardless of the industry in which they work.

So if you inspire others to want to take action, you are leading. It's that simple.

Implicit in this definition is that the following three things which are often *associated* with leaders do not actually *make you* a leader:

- **Your personality does not make you a leader.** A big personality does not make you a leader (though it may make you charismatic) any more than a reserved personality holds you back from being one.

- **Your title does not make you a leader.** Audiences may be more inclined to listen to you if you have CEO or something impressive in your title, but they will feel no compunction to follow you because of what is printed on your business card.

- **Your direct reports do not make you a leader.** Just because you have many people in your organization who must act on your direction does not mean they will choose to follow you; those managers who rely on organizational clout soon find their people leave for other teams or other organizations.

If you can inspire others to follow – to act upon your ideas – you are leading. At The Humphrey Group we believe this ability to lead is not something you are born with but rather something that you can and do purposefully develop. Choosing to lead is a choice and carries with it benefits and challenges. The work of leading is just that – work – and it requires deliberate practice before it becomes instinctive and second nature.

In my role as an executive coach, I help our clients develop one of the most crucial skills that leaders use: the ability to communicate with others.

The Link between Leadership and Communication

Communication is the only way that leaders can and do inspire others to act. As a leader, you should consciously approach every interaction as an opportunity to influence and inspire your audiences. You must persuade others to act on the ideas you believe in during your phone calls, meetings, presentations, formal speeches, and in all the interactions that make up your day-to-day. Your power is derived not from your title, but from your ability to influence and inspire others to act.

When I spoke to leaders in my interviews, the importance of communication was a common refrain. Here are a few examples of what I heard:

Susan Uchida, Vice President of Learning at the Royal Bank of Canada, described it this way:

Communication is a critical tool [for leaders] because it's the way you connect with people and you inspire them and it helps them understand what your perspective is, and it helps them … translate it to their own beliefs [rather] than their own actions. So, the choice of words, the style of communication really can be very meaningful.

Here's Dane Jensen, CEO of Performance Coaching, a Toronto-based leadership development firm. Dane, a former management consultant, had this to say about leadership:

Leaders get other people excited about reaching their full potential. [Communication] is how you ply your trade as a leader. It is the way you connect with another human being.

Here's Bruno Sperduti, Executive Vice President, Rental Management at FirstService Residential:

Leadership is about creating an action, changing behavior toward a goal … [and] words create actions in the first place. [Leadership] has to be all about communication.

Leadership *is* all about communication. Leading by example is essential, but actions without words limit your ability to reach your audiences. It's your words that help your audience understand the ideas and beliefs that shape your actions.

Creating believers – the true task of leaders – requires a day-in-and-day-out commitment to thinking clearly and persuasively, and sharing this thinking with others. Every conversation is an opportunity not merely to inform but also to inspire. Here's what the author and motivational speaker Simon Sinek says in his book *Start with Why*:

Great leaders … are able to inspire people to act. Those who are able to inspire give people a sense of purpose or belonging that has little to do with any incentive or benefit to be gained. Those who truly lead are able to create a following of people who act not because they are swayed, but because they were inspired. For those who are inspired, the motivation to act is deeply personal.[1]

So if you want to lead, your focus must be on shaping the beliefs of your audience because this is the step you must take to create a long-term commitment to action. But how do you do this?

An ideal starting point is to begin thinking consciously about your communication – and how others around you are communicating. What words do you use when you want to shape the beliefs of those you wish to inspire? In short, what exactly is the language of leadership?

START BY CONSCIOUSLY LOOKING AT LANGUAGE THROUGH THE LENS OF LEADERSHIP

Sometimes it's important to stop and reflect on the language we use to communicate. How you do this depends entirely on your perspective. If you were assessing the effectiveness of an expert, you might choose to evaluate his ability to convey knowledge with clarity. If you were to assess the effectiveness of a grade-seven teacher, you might evaluate his ability to hold a room of 30 children with short attention spans and engage them in learning. If you were assessing the effectiveness of a motivational speaker, you might look at how much energy he could bring into a room.

But if you were assessing leaders, there could be only one litmus test: Does the way they communicate inspire their audiences to act? And, do the words they use to communicate their ideas help or hinder their ability to lead others?

SUMMARY

Rick could have stood up and droned on about "KPIs" (Key Performance Indicators), talked about "Six Sigma manufacturing strategies," or discussed "margin compression." He chose instead to focus on leading inspirationally by telling a story that would resonate with his listeners and help them understand both what their company was facing and the path they needed to follow. He told his story not with corporate-speak but with language that was plain and powerful.

Leadership – the ability to inspire others to act – is not an innate ability. It's not the result of a big title or an advanced degree. Rather, it is a skill that is developed over time and honed in every interaction.

As you read through this book, I ask you to do so with this mindset. Now, with that in mind, let's look at jargon and its implications for your goal of leading every time you speak.

NOTES

1. Simon Sinek, *Start with Why: How Great Leaders Inspire Everyone to Take Action* (New York: Portfolio, 2011), 8.

2

THE (FEW) BENEFITS OF JARGON

Imagine you are sitting at your desk when a package arrives for you. You haven't been expecting a package, so you look at it with interest. You notice that there is a waybill with a description of the contents. You look closely at the waybill, which says:

> This package contains the list of reasons to use jargon.

Intrigued, you get a knife and prepare to open the package, but just before you start cutting the tape you notice a large warning label on the other side. In bright red letters it says:

> WARNING: Contents may prove harmful to your leadership! Open and use with great care.

You continue cutting the tape, open the package and find...this chapter.

Why does a chapter on the benefits of jargon come to you with a warning label? Simple: because though there are some benefits to using acronyms, technical terminology, and corporate-speak, such benefits are almost always overestimated and used to justify the continued use of words that fail to inspire others.

You are reading this book because you want to communicate as a leader. As you seek to influence and inspire, there are two beneficial reasons to use jargon: for expediency (to speed up communications) and to foster a shared identity (to forge culture and identity).

This chapter will look at this kind of jargon and the situations where it can be used to your benefit; this chapter will also point out the possible things that can go wrong if you do use it. But first, let's see where these terms sit on the Jargon Spectrum.

WHERE DO "EXPEDIENCY" AND "SHARED IDENTITY" JARGON SIT ON THE JARGON SPECTRUM?

Both expediency jargon and shared identity jargon sit on the left side of the Jargon Spectrum (see Figure 2.1). At their best, both types of jargon can prove useful for leaders because they shorten the time they need to convey ideas and they create a common language that can bind audiences together. Thus, they are deemed useful.

Yet, leaders must be cautious that the benefits of these "useful" terms are not trumped by the potential consequences of using them, namely, confusing and excluding members of their audiences. The same acronym that cuts down on time can alienate a new employee; the same

Figure 2.1 The Jargon Spectrum.

buzzword that conjures up shared understanding can confuse those who attach a different meaning to it.

EFFICIENCY: JARGON THAT SERVES AS "VERBAL SHORTHAND"

As a leader, the most compelling reason for you to use jargon is efficiency. When you and your audience have a shared understanding of acronyms, technological terminology, or conceptual language, they allow you to save time and avoid redundant explanations.

Acronyms are perhaps the most common example of efficiency-driven jargon. They allow speakers to introduce complex terminology that would be repetitive if "spelled out." Think of a CEO at her annual general meeting speaking to analysts. Instead of saying "earnings per share," she can say "EPS." Instead of saying "earnings before interest, taxes, depreciation, and amortization," she can say "EBITDA." Instead of saying "compound annual growth rate," she can say "CAGR."

Here's Steve Reid, board member at Silver Standard and Eldorado Gold, and the former Chief Operating Officer at Goldcorp, one of the world's largest gold producers, on the use of acronyms:

> People use it. They use it for speed. You've got a very long description of some organization or some project or something, you abbreviate it.

Here's Marcella Szel, former railway executive and now Chair of the Board of Translink, British Columbia's transit operator:

> It's just a short form of talking. As long as everyone in the room understands what you're talking about, it makes a conversation shorter.

Not all acronyms serve the same purpose, however. Today, John King is CEO of Gemma Communication, a contact center company, but earlier in his career he served in the Canadian Armed Forces, where he held the rank of captain. John talked to me about the two categories of acronyms in the military – formal and informal:

> Acronyms are very big. Both formal and informal.
> A formal acronym would be something specific and official, like saying XO rather than "executive officer."

An informal acronym would be SNAFU.[1]

There are benefits to both [formal and informal] because informal acronyms create a sense of affiliation among members, whereas formal acronyms and formal jargon are more for expediency.

You know it's easier to remember. In the military, the intent is to make things a drill. There's a lot of memorization from steps of battle procedure to orders format, be it . . . the situation, mission, execution, service support command and [so on]. You memorize [the acronyms] and you never forget. Then everyone has a common body of knowledge.

As John explains, when everyone has done the work of memorizing and learning the definitions of acronyms, communication becomes faster. This allows people in combat to make decisions more quickly.

Now, here's that warning label again: for expediency jargon to work, everyone has to have the same understanding of what the acronyms mean.

Here's Steve Reid again:

There's somewhat of a valid reason to initially use jargon . . . but I think very quickly, you've got to get away from it . . . if you're using some sort of acronym or something, you've got to be able to understand when you use it and when you don't. You don't use that acronym that's used for a very small elite team and . . . then go and speak in a broader audience and you still use it because you're conditioned to using it.

As Steve and others pointed out to me in our interviews, that's all too often what happens. Speakers routinely presume their audiences understand what the terminology they are using stands for.

Here's a real world example of the danger of acronyms outweighing the benefits of expediency. The story was shared with me by Michael Morrow, a Partner and Senior Managing Director in the accounting firm Deloitte. Michael's expertise lies in mergers and acquisitions:

I was in a meeting yesterday [in] which [people were] talking about MD, which I interpreted in a different way than what was actually being talked about.

MD is an organization that we acquired four years ago called Managerial Design. In consulting, at least the circles that I run in, MD stands for Managerial Design. So, someone else in [this meeting] was talking about MD and I assumed that it was Managerial Design.

In fact, as I later understood, it [was used as an acronym for] Monitor Deloitte, another organization that we purchased [but] which I would always call Monitor. But [after the acquisition] they co-branded the name and it is now Monitor Deloitte.

Both Michael and the others attending the meeting were working under the mistaken assumption that the other side knew what *their* definition of MD was. Neither party bothered to confirm it. Michael's story is by no means unique and exemplifies the ramifications of using shorthand without a shared understanding of its underlying meaning.

So is there value in using jargon as shorthand? Ultimately yes, but with the caveat that you must be sure your audience knows what you mean. More on this in the next chapter.

⌘

SIGNALING CREDIBILITY

Another benefit of jargon that leaders should be aware of is how people use it to signal expertise and establish credibility.

As the world moves toward a knowledge economy, the "products" that companies sell are increasingly ideas – and the people who will implement them.

But how do you "test" an idea? How do you quickly evaluate individuals and assess their capabilities? One way to do so is to listen carefully to the words they use. For this reason, using jargon can quickly allow speakers to establish their expertise and credibility.

In some instances it becomes a requirement for doing business. Robert Gouley is a Senior Analyst at OMERS Capital Markets,[2] a major Canadian pension fund. He told me:

[The ability to speak the language of your profession] is almost like a minimum standard to be able to do the job. People want you to speak their language before they will engage with you. Sometimes, even if you can say it simpler, within that defined group that all speaks the same language they want you to speak it in their language. They don't want you to say it a different way.

Emily Alonzo is Project Manager, Marketing and Innovation at Bell Media, a leading Canadian TV, radio, and digital media company. She told me, "If you're using jargon, you're in the club. You are inside and you can pass the basics." In signaling your credibility through language, you are signaling a deeper understanding of broader concepts that are expressed as one word.

Yet, leaders must be cautious of relying on jargon to gain entry "into the club." While jargon can establish your credibility, simply using the *lingua franca* of your profession or company can undermine you if you aren't confident in what it is you are actually saying.

CREATING A SHARED CULTURE

A final benefit of jargon is that its use allows a group to forge a shared cultural or social identity. It turns out there is sound research to back up this idea. Dr Kimberly Noels is an Adjunct Professor in the Department of Educational Psychology at the University of Alberta. Noels's focus of study is the social psychology of language, applied linguistics, and cultural psychology and how they relate to intercultural relations and communication.

I came across Noels while reading an article entitled "Why NHL Players Speak in Clichés during Interviews and How 'Hockeyspeak' Developed Over Generations" in Canada's *National Post* newspaper. The article focuses on NHL players who spout the same meaningless jargon and clichés in post-game interviews, like "we gave 110%" or "we just have to get better every day." Noels explains the value behind this kind of common language:

It's called convergence.... We have a tendency when we communicate with other people to converge to the same style [of speech] that they have.... That can be in things like how fast we speak or what kind of vocabulary choices we make.

Noels goes on to describe the benefits of convergence:

In part it helps us to exchange information with other people.... The more similar we are, the easier it is to understand each other. It also helps with liking. The more similar we are to each other it creates a kind of unity.

It creates a common ground or understanding of what you're talking about, but also who we are. We share this common interest or identity.[3]

This common ground and strengthened bond are powerful reasons to create and use a common set of words. As Steve Reid points out, "Language does build teams. It does build an inclusive inner circle...."

When done right, language which can be meaningless to outsiders conjures up a common, deeper meaning that resonates with and unites listeners. Here's an example of that, as related to me by Les Dakens, the former CHRO (that's Chief Human Resources Officer) for Maple Leaf Foods and Canadian National Rail:

Jargon allows you to be part of a unique group. It can have a positive benefit... and let me give you an example. In the railway business, to be called an outstanding railroader – you couldn't give me a better compliment. What's a railroader? That's someone who really, really understands the business and is recognized as just outstanding in their field. That kind of jargon works because [it may not mean anything to you] but within that culture that's a big deal. In that situation, it actually helps your leadership of that group....

Leaders only derive the benefit of a shared identity when they use jargon that *the whole group understands*. Dr Greg Wells is Assistant Professor at the University of Toronto and Associate Scientist at SickKids Hospital. He is also a coach to world-class athletes. He explained that when it comes to shared identity jargon:

One way of thinking about it is internal versus external. When I'm talking about the jargon used within swimming, or the jargon within the cancer department and SickKids, those terms, those words, the way of speaking...enhances the ability of that group to operate efficiently, effectively, more powerfully and then also create culture which is amazing.

But there is (again) a dangerous flip side to this as well, which Greg went on to describe:

But if you're then trying to go and use the [ideas and language] gleaned from those incredible groups to inspire people into action...if we start to use those terms that we have developed within these tight-knit cultures to inspire people [who are not part of that group], you have the opposite effect.

In fact, though it pains me to admit it, we have our own internal/external jargon at The Humphrey Group. We use terminology internally and with clients that carries with it meaning that is specific to our company and mission. Yet, we know that we must take pains – particularly when communicating externally – to define that jargon.

For example, if you attend one of our workshops or take an executive coaching program with us, you will hear us talk about "inspiring" your audience. Many participants initially recoil at this term. Upon hearing this word, one executive whom I was coaching said to me, "I hope you don't expect me to turn into Tony Robbins and get people to walk over hot coals. I run a quality assurance group, not a cult."

After a good laugh I assured him I had no such ambitions for him, and that I defined *inspiration* as the ability to communicate ideas that lead others to make the choice to act (rather than because they are compelled to do so). In some cases, I told him, such inspiration could be quite mundane, for example to be inspired to complete a project on time, while in other instances it could be on a grander but still practical scale – such as inspiring a team to stick with a company through a downturn.

We came back to this definition of inspirational communication frequently in the coaching program. As he became more comfortable with the term, he began to use it and now, he told me, he uses it consistently. "I look at how to use every interaction to inspire my audience."

Creating a shared culture and identity through language is desirable for leaders. Take care, though, not to share such language with other audiences, and to take the time to help those not yet part of the group to understand the words that they will need to know if they are to belong.

SUMMARY

There are positive benefits to be had from the careful definition and use of jargon. It can create a common language, a shared identity, and a stronger shared culture. To achieve these benefits, again, speakers must be sure they have defined the words and that the audience shares that understanding.

NOTES

1. If you don't know SNAFU, it stands for "situation normal, all f*&*! up".
2. Ontario Municipal Employees Retirement System.
3. Chris O'Leary, "Why NHL Players Speak in Clichés during Interviews and How 'Hockeyspeak' Developed Over Generations," *National Post*, March 22, 2015, http://news.nationalpost.com/2015/03/22/why-nhl-players-speak-in-cliches-during-interviews-and-how-hockeyspeak-developed-over-generations/.

3

ASSUMPTION-
DRIVEN
JARGON

In the early 2000s, my team and I were delivering a Speaking as a
Leader workshop to a group of senior bankers who collectively ran
a large personal and commercial banking business unit. Prior to the
workshop, we had met with the sponsoring executive to discuss the
presentations that each of the eight participants would be preparing
using the communications methodology we would teach in the workshop. This approach would show them how to move from "information to inspiration" and deliver a message that would engage and inspire
their audience.

The executive told us that this was an ideal opportunity for
each member of his senior team to prepare a presentation that would
elaborate on how the company's new globalization strategy would
enable them to drive profitable growth.

When the workshop got underway, the participants expressed
excitement about the exercise. They spoke about their passion for
the globalization strategy, their collective commitment to it, and the

sense of unity they shared in "going global" after years of being locally focused. At the end of the first day participants worked on the outlines for their presentations, which they were to present the next day to their colleagues – and to their boss.

The team didn't know it yet, but they were all operating under a common, but mistaken assumption: that they had a common definition of the word "globalization."

The next morning, the presentations began. First up was Geoffrey,[1] a passionate ex-consultant who had been impressing everyone with his drive and enthusiasm ever since joining the bank two years earlier.

"We will realize the promise of globalization," he said, "by focusing on accretive acquisitions in underserved retail banking geographies like the Caribbean." His presentation went on to outline a high-level acquisition strategy for building the bank's profile in new markets.

When he finished, there were some looks of concern between many of the participants. Yet, no one said anything as the next presenter came to the front of the room.

"Ummm...so this is a bit of a different take," began Ruth, a well-regarded retail banker who had worked her way up from teller to vice president.

"When I think globalization, I actually think about tailoring our offerings to global customers. For example, in the United States we are seeing many banks achieve great success catering to the underserved Hispanic demographics; we know here in our Canadian market we have many new immigrants from India and East Asia who are not having their needs met, and I believe going global means helping attract their business." Her presentation laid out some initial thoughts on how they could pursue this course of action.

Again, silence and looks around the room. Could both these presentations really be discussing the same global strategy?

Then Brad got up and began with, "Well, I'm getting nervous here...because my take on globalization is entirely different, but here goes nothing...."

In the end, the eight executives each presented compelling – yet radically different – visions of what it meant to "go global." The executive was as shocked as the participants by these variations. How could they have been so united in their belief in the strategy and yet end up with such fundamentally different pictures of what it meant?

The answer was simple: the executive who led the group *assumed* everyone knew what he was talking about when he directed them to pursue a globalization strategy. In his mind, globalization meant using their strong domestic banking business to fund acquisitions outside of Canada. But he failed to share that definition and no one asked him to do so. The result was that each executive was left to interpret and define what the term meant – leading to eight very different, and competing, paths to execution.

The good news is that once these competing definitions surfaced, a common understanding emerged. The executives were then able to chart a course towards their shared goal, and that course guided them successfully forward in the years ahead.

This example clearly shows that assuming everyone understands a concept can create very awkward moments for a leader. As the popular saying goes, when you assume, you make an ASS out of U and ME. This is particularly true when it comes to jargon: in this case the use of globalization and the failure to define it. Speakers far too often make the assumption that the audience knows what their jargon means. The result is confusion, lack of agreement, or potentially even agreement with something that may not be valid.

MAKING ASSUMPTIONS ON THE JARGON SPECTRUM

Jargon born of assumptions sits in the middle of the Jargon Spectrum (see Figure 3.1). This type of jargon can affect leaders in a range of ways: from receiving benign responses (in instances where not "getting it" doesn't lead to problems) to ineffective ones (when audiences take no action or take the wrong action because they did not understand the meaning of the term).

Jargon that stems from assumptions is rarely intentional; instead, it is a product of either failing to consider the audience or failing to

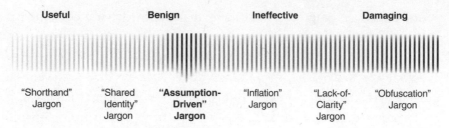

Figure 3.1 The Jargon Spectrum.

define the terminology being used. Not all assumptions are created equally, and not all have the same outcome.

THE CURSE OF KNOWLEDGE

Why do bright people continue to make the mistake of assuming the audience knows what the jargon they use means? One reason to explain this is the concept known as the "curse of knowledge." This concept was first described to me by Dane Jensen, CEO of Performance Coaching:

> The curse of knowledge is ... a cognitive bias rooted in the notion that once you know something, it is pretty much impossible to remember what it was like when you didn't know that thing. When you are a CEO and you have been on quarterly earnings calls for 10 years and you have this richly nuanced view and understanding of what "shareholder value creation" means to all of these institutional shareholders and activist investors and board members, when you use the words, "shareholder value creation," there is a huge amount of context and richness that is running through your head that is embedded in those three words. Unfortunately, because of that cognitive bias, it's very hard for the same CEO to put themselves in the shoes of a frontline employee or a frontline manager.
>
> When [those employees or that manager] hear those three words, they literally hear nothing. It sounds like empty management speak. They're thinking, okay, "shareholder value creation," here we go again. That's basically slang for cost-cutting....

In his outstanding book, *The Sense of Style,* Steven Pinker expands on the consequences of the curse of knowledge for writers (though the same conclusions certainly apply to speakers):

> …the Curse of Knowledge: a difficulty in imagining what it is like for someone else not to know something that you know.

The curse of knowledge is the single best explanation I know of why good people write bad prose. It simply doesn't occur to the writer that her readers don't know what she knows – that they haven't mastered the patois of her guild, can't divine the missing steps that seem too obvious to mention, have no way to visualize a scene that to her is as clear as day. And so she doesn't bother to explain the jargon, or spell out the logic, or supply the necessary detail.[2]

What can be done about this curse? Pinker again:

> A better way to exorcise the curse of knowledge is to be aware of specific pitfalls that it sets in your path. There's one that everyone is at least vaguely aware of: the use of jargon, abbreviations and technical vocabulary. Every human pastime – music, cooking, sports, art, theoretical physics – develops an argot to spare its enthusiasts from having to say or type a long-winded description every time they refer to a familiar concept in each other's company. The problem is that as we become proficient at our job or hobby we come to use these catchwords so often that they flow out of our fingers automatically, and we forget that our readers may not be members of the clubhouse in which we learned them.[3]

Self-awareness is indeed the starting point for dealing with assumption-driven jargon. Take a moment to assess your own language and to see if you are guilty of using assumption-driven jargon.

What kind of assumptions might you be making and what jargon are you likely using if you are in the grasp of the curse of knowledge?

ACRONYMS AND OTHER SHORTHAND

The most common assumption speakers make is that their jargon is understood by the whole audience.

In Chapter 2, I discussed how this kind of shorthand allows speakers to save time and get to the point with audiences who understand what they are referring to.

Yet, far too often speakers make the assumption that the audience knows what their verbal shorthand means, when in fact the audience does not. The result: their ideas can be "lost in translation."

Here's what Guy Jarvis, Chief Commercial Officer at Enbridge, told me about acronyms and assumptions:

> While industry acronyms…can be effective internally…the flip side is [they can be] one of our industry's biggest problems when we try to go communicate externally.
>
> I know what we do is very technical, but we as an industry have done a terrible job of taking what at times can be technical or complex and converting it into a message that resonates with the public. We get up there and we talk about DRA and ILIs and HCAs and the public's eyes are just glazing over.

Guy's point is that it is all well and good to use technical terminology internally, but you can really hurt yourself if you assume that your external audience – that is, those outside of your company and industry – will understand it.

It's important to know that members of an audience rarely, if ever, put their hands up and ask for a definition of an acronym or a term they don't understand. In some cases, they may even have a *legitimate, yet different understanding* of what your acronym means.

In Chapter 2 I shared a story related to me by Michael Morrow at Deloitte, who told me how two different sets of executives at a meeting had entirely different understandings of what MD stood for – some understood it to mean Monitor Deloitte and others to mean Managerial Design. In fact, double-meaning[4] acronyms are not uncommon and fall into three categories:

- One acronym with two distinct expansions, each of which refers to the same term:
  - ACT (popular cognitive modeling tool), stands for both
    - Atomic Components of Thought
    - Adaptive Character of Thought;
  - CPM-GOMS (tool from human–computer interaction), CPM stands for both
    - cognitive, perceptual, motor
    - critical path method;
- One acronym with two distinct expansions, each of which refers to completely different things:
  - CSR
    - Customer service representative
    - Corporate social responsibility;
  - NSA
    - National Security Agency
    - National Security Act;
- One acronym with distinctive meanings when used across cultures:
  - NIC
    - (In English) New Iraqi Corps, 2003 intended description of U.S.-trained Iraqi forces
    - (In Arabic) a colorful term for fornication.

These examples show that the acronym you choose might have a meaning that is entirely different from the one you assumed your audience knew. But what if that acronym had three other different meanings? What if it had five? Or eight?

Try this test: here are three acronyms that you may know how to expand. Each has at least three different expansions. Try each and see how many different expansions you can write down. Then consult the answers below and see how many actually exist for each.

> P&L
>
> IPO
>
> ROI

And now the answers:

I have found five distinct expansions for P&L:

- Profit & loss;
- Peace and love;
- Performance & luxury;
- Production & logistics;
- Policy & liaison.

IPO has at least eight distinct expansions:

- Initial public offering;
- Illustrative purposes only;
- International procurement/purchasing office;
- Investing pays off (courtesy of Merrill Lynch);
- Internal purchase order;
- Individual pays own;
- Initial purchase order;
- Independent program oversight.

And ROI has *at least* 21 distinct expansions:

- Return on investment;
- Region of interest;
- Republic of Ireland;
- Release of information;
- Rate of interest;
- Report of investigation;

- Reactive oxygen intermediate;
- Registration of interest;
- Radius of influence;
- Rules of interaction;
- Risk of incarceration;
- Record of invention;
- Return on integrity;
- Realm of influence;
- Report on investigation;
- Remote operator interface;
- Read only information;
- Range operating instruction;
- Route of ingress;
- Risk of infection;
- Report on industry.

Now consider the implications – if you were to use any of these acronyms as industry shorthand, what are the odds that

    A. Your audience would know how to expand it?
    B. Their expansion would match yours?

As this exercise shows, the odds of both of A and B being consistently true when you use acronyms may be far lower than you assumed.

Like me, you may have been surprised by the number of distinct expansions that exist for each of the three test acronyms. I certainly didn't know them. So how did I find out about the expansions for P&L, ROI, and IPO? I found them thanks to a brilliant (and somewhat frightening) website I discovered while researching this book: www.acronymfinder.com. Here's how the website defines its *raison d'être*:

With more than 1,000,000 human-edited definitions, Acronym Finder is the world's largest and most comprehensive dictionary of acronyms, abbreviations, and initialisms. Combined with the Acronym Attic, Acronym Finder contains more than 5 million acronyms and abbreviations.

Try looking up some of your favorite acronyms to see what other expansions exist. Or, better yet, try making up an acronym – you will be shocked at how it may actually stand for something.

ASSUMING UNDERSTANDING OF COMPLEX CONCEPTS

Assuming your audience knows how to expand an acronym you are using is one thing. Assuming they understand the meaning you attach to a more complex piece of jargon is another. As Dane Jensen remarks above, the use of "shareholder value creation" was meaningful to him but sounded like corporate-babble to his audience, proving that it is the buzzwords and conceptual words that are most vulnerable to unfounded assumptions about audience understanding.

Now, a caveat: in this chapter we will operate under the assumption that you actually do have a clear definition for the jargon you are using, and that you are choosing to use it to derive the benefits discussed in Chapter 2. (In Chapter 5 we will look at a more damning, yet regular occurrence – the use of jargon as a *substitute for clarity*.)

In our work at The Humphrey Group, we find that when it comes to jargon, speakers consistently make two mistakes:

1. They overestimate their audiences' understanding of their terminology.
2. They underestimate the results of making those inaccurate assumptions.

The reality is that many leaders actually do have well-defined definitions in their own mind for the terminology they use when they are speaking. Often, when asked to explain their terminology, they do so quite happily and readily. But, they may well assume that the audience shares their understanding and the result is they leave listeners in the dark. This can have significant consequences.

Bruce Derraugh, Chief Operating Officer at FirstOnSite Restoration, a disaster recovery company, shared some of those consequences with me. He told me a story about what can happen when a speaker mistakenly believes his audience knows what he means.

A number of years ago I was at a town hall [meeting] where two large companies were being integrated. The CEO was presenting the direction of the business and what really needed to happen for the integration to be successful.

He spoke only of the company that he came from and did not speak to any of the real benefits from the merger. He also emphasized that costs were going to have to be cut.

Yet he didn't define what cost cutting would look like. That led to the people in the organization that had been taken over to assume the CEO did not care about their business and was likely to draw job cuts from their organization.

That was not the case at all that happened. People were taken out of both organizations, but the fundamental cost cuts would really come through real estate consolidation, changes to the overall business model, and they actually needed the new organization more than they needed the old, existing business. Unfortunately ... [the company] lost some of the top people in that business because of unclear communication about the direction of change, which led people to assume the worst.

In this example, the CEO *knew* what he meant by cost cutting. He *knew* that he would need people from both companies. Yet, he assumed that his audience would know as well, to his detriment.

Imagine the difference in that story if the leader had said where the costs would be cut, how the organization needed talent from both companies, and that there were benefits to be had for all through the integration of the businesses. Instead, jargon – and assumptions – led to an exodus.

BEWARE GROUP ASSUMPTIONS AND THE POWER OF THE COLLECTIVE

Jargon can get really out of hand when a group collectively begins using it. Our desire as humans to belong is tremendously powerful. Because language is a signifier of belonging, few individuals feel comfortable putting their hand up and asking others to explain what they mean. When people join groups, they simply begin using the terminology and hope to develop an understanding of it. Gradually, they create their own definition, which may or may not be the same as their colleagues. When others join the group, the process is repeated. Over time, the group derives a sense of shared identity through the use of this terminology, but the group rarely questions whether the assumptions behind their words are the same.

Here's Steve Reid on this subject:

> You see numerous examples where a meeting is going on, some slang or internal language is being used and three quarters of the room gets it and a quarter doesn't and yet the meeting continues. The people who don't get it don't say anything because they don't want to look bad.

In my experience this is typical, and the consequences can be significant. Some years ago I was teaching a workshop to a group of executives at a large manufacturing company in Calgary, Alberta. We were talking language and many of the participants in the group were challenging my suggestion that jargon was undermining their ability to be heard and to inspire others to act.

One said: "Yes we use a lot of industry-speak, but we're a tight team who have been working together for a long time and we understand each other."

Another: "It's useful because it lets us save time and speak a common language."

A third spoke up: "Everyone here knows what I'm talking about when I use those words."

I realized that I wasn't going to persuade any of them through direct argument, so I decided to put a challenge to the group. I told them that we would try a little test. I would select one buzzword from their vision and strategy document and they would write down their definitions. They would then read out these definitions and see what kind of consistency they had.

They agreed. I chose the term "top decile," which was their stated goal for company performance five years out. As executives began to read aloud their definitions, it became clear that their understandings of top decile, and consequently of success, varied radically.

We tried again, with another term – "culture of continuous improvement." Again, the definitions were not consistent. We looked at a third term – "operationalizing efficiency" – with the same result. Finally, one of the executives put up his hand and spoke, "OK, I'll just go ahead and say it: the emperor isn't wearing any clothes."[5]

The uncomfortable laughs in the room gave way to meaningful discussion. Why was this happening? Why had no one said anything? What were the impacts? And how long had this been going on?

Just like the banking executives who were pursuing globalization, the manufacturing executives had made the mistake of assuming that they shared a collective set of definitions for terms they were using. Over time these assumptions had become ingrained into their work and their communication. While they enjoyed the benefits they derived from using a common, exclusive language, they underestimated the ramifications of having different definitions for those terms.

⚬⚬⚬

SUMMARY

In Chapter 2, I outlined the benefits of jargon: expediency in delivering a message, shared social identity in a workplace, and the ability to capture a set of ideas in a unique word or set of words. Yet, those benefits can be realized only if the speakers and their audience collectively have the same understanding of what the jargon actually means. Sadly, this is rarely the case, and any benefits to be gained by jargon are wiped out by the misunderstandings that ensue when speakers make unfounded assumptions about the language they choose to use.

Notes

1. All names have been changed.
2. Steven Pinker, *The Sense of Style: The Thinking Person's Guide to Writing in the 21st Century* (New York: Viking, 2014), 59, 61.
3. Ibid., 63.
4. English Language and Usage, http://english.stackexchange.com/questions/97710/double-acronym-acronyms-that-stand-for-two-things-simultaneously.
5. This story refers to Hans Christian Andersen's tale of weavers who create for the emperor a new suit of clothes which is invisible to those who are stupid or incompetent. When the emperor shows off his new "outfit" no one dares to say a thing until a child remarks, "But he isn't wearing anything at all," https://en.wikipedia.org/wiki/The_Emperor's_New_Clothes.

4

INFLATION
JARGON

The television series *House of Lies* is a true guilty pleasure for anyone who works in management consulting or who hires management consultants. If you haven't yet seen the show, it stars Don Cheadle as Marty Khan who leads a "pod" of self-loathing, high-priced, low-value management consultants based in Los Angeles.

In the first episode of season 1, Khan is brought into a surprise meeting with a major financial institution which has been an important client. The senior executive leading the meeting has a bone to pick with Khan and confronts him with, "You're the mad genius we're paying all this money for? Well, why don't you just tell us what you're thinking. Go."

Khan first tries to flatter the client, unsuccessfully. Then he tries to ask the client for *his* opinion, which also fails to impress. In desperate straits, Khan holds up a sign with his trump card. It reads, "Use Indecipherable Jargon" (this is one of the show's greatest tropes – Khan freezing the scene and talking directly to the audience, letting the viewers in on the idiocy of what he is doing).

Then he starts talking: "Because the pod remains convinced there is a burning platform but we just don't have the bandwidth to go into a black factory and blow out the paradigms with a white paper."

Everyone I talk to about this moment in this episode – and believe me, *everyone I know* in the consulting world watches this show – has two reactions to Khan's jargon. First, that it's absolutely hilarious. And, second, that it is uncomfortably accurate.

The truth is, the kind of language that Khan uses to bamboozle his client is not solely heard in the domain of satirical shows like *House of Lies*. And it's not restricted to management consultants, despite the easy target they present. If you spend any time in a workplace, you are bound to hear versions of Marty Khan speaking in inflated corporate-speak, using terms that few understand.

What's going on here? Why does this happen? Because using this kind of language has one particular payoff – at first blush, it sounds impressive. And it creates a sense of importance that can benefit the speaker. Geoffrey Nunberg, a University of California, Berkeley linguist, says that specialized language was invented for organizational purposes, and as a specialized language understood only by insiders it gave white-collar workers a sense "that the work experience was somehow different and grander than the experience of ordinary life."[1]

In addition to building up their own egos, speakers who use inflated words may be trying to show others that they are brilliant. Here's what Almis Ledas, Chief Operating Officer at Enstream (a Canadian mobile payments company), says on this topic:

> While sometimes new terms [jargon] are needed to express more complex thoughts, there may be people who equate the use of jargon with a higher level thinking, which is clearly not the case .... Jargon may be a way for some people to try to elevate the complexity of what they are trying to express.

Anne Sado, President of George Brown College in Toronto, makes the same point:

> Sometimes I have found ... people use [jargon] because it's a way of letting you know that they have some level of knowledge ....

I listen to people and there are some days when I just can't understand all the acronyms. Some people literally speak in acronyms and I sit there and I say, "What does that mean?" They may be trying to illustrate how knowledgeable they are – although when questioned, they often can't tell you what any given acronym stands for. It could be they use them for convenience, or maybe they're staying a notch above you with the knowledge…just a "bit unreachable."

One profession that is notorious for using this kind of language – and for creating distance with its audiences – is the legal profession. As part of my research, I spoke with members of the legal profession about the use of jargon and its impact on lawyers and their clients. I met with Geoff Lyster, a Partner in the global law firm Fasken Martineau DuMoulin LLP. Geoff is an experienced mergers and acquisitions lawyer who has always impressed me with the clarity of his thinking and the absence of jargon when he discusses legal issues. When I asked Geoff about unnecessarily technical language in the legal profession, he agreed it was a real issue:

Lawyers are notorious for using legalese and heretofores and wheretofores and all the stuff that nobody else understands.

Geoff explained that this process of using legally inflated language begins in the first days of law school:

I remember [in] the first week of law school we had a professor who gave us a list of 20 words…. We had to write down what they meant or what [we] thought they meant and [we] got maybe three or four [of the terms right]. I remember quantum, [which] just means amount, was one of the ones I got wrong. Today, the term is so second nature to me it seems strange that someone might not know what it means. But, of course, many non-lawyers wouldn't.

Geoff explained why many young lawyers fall into this trap of using jargon to project credibility:

As a junior, and I fell into this trap for sure, you can hide behind the cloak of [the expert language] and perhaps try to project greater experience than you have. But as you get more senior and have greater confidence in your knowledge and abilities, then you can say goodbye to that and speak like a normal person.

Geoff went on to describe how the legal profession was aware that this kind of language was hurting its ability to serve clients, and how lawyers are working to change the language they use:

I know there's a push at the law schools, and through the Professional Legal Training Course, which is the bar training course in BC, and regular courses from Continuing Legal Education, for use of plain language. It's a cry by the market saying, "Come on, it's unnecessary, use words that we understand" .... For most of our communications, and certainly communications with our clients, there's no need for it.

As Geoff, Almis, and Anne all point out, just because you *can* make something sound more complex than it is, does not mean you should. Using inflation jargon does allow speakers to project expertise and credibility, but such benefits are outweighed by the annoyance and lack of understanding felt by the audiences who hear it.

INFLATION ON THE JARGON SPECTRUM

For these reasons, language used to inflate the importance of what is being said sits on the middle-to-right side of the Jargon Spectrum (see Figure 4.1).

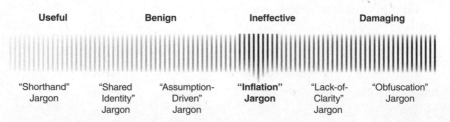

Figure 4.1 The Jargon Spectrum.

Inflation jargon is "ineffective" because it undermines leadership: at best it confuses audiences, and at worst it leads to the speaker being viewed as a blowhard. Our first reaction as a listener might be to say, "I don't get what that person is saying, so clearly I must lack the knowledge/sophistication/intelligence/MBA/consulting background to really understand the wisdom that is undoubtedly being conveyed to me in this moment."

Leaders should be on the lookout for this kind of jargon – both so they can avoid feeling insecure when it is used and so they can avoid its use themselves. Here is a look at various subcategories of inflation jargon, and why each has no place in the language of leadership.

The Better Version

One of the most common types of inflation jargon is what I call the "better version." You have heard better-version jargon used wherever a perfectly good word or phrase is deemed to be unsuitable for the audience and is replaced by a more impressive, yet substantively similar word or phrase. In her book *Word Up!* Marcia Riefer Johnston has a whole chapter on this kind of linguistic fluffing. She writes:

> Still waiting for that promotion? Try talking like a boss .... People take you more seriously when you use fuzzier language ....
>
> Is your department overworked? You don't need people. You need resources .... Need an extra chair? You could get one. Then again you could procure one .... Don't tell people what to do; give them action items. Don't make plans; negotiate logistics. Don't prepare; do legwork. Don't get people to agree with you; get them to buy in. First, though, triangulate (don't bounce) your ideas off them.[2]

Want more examples? Consider the word pairs in Table 4.1.

What is the difference between the words on the left side of the table and the words on the right? The answer: very little. The words on the right contain more letters. They sound more impressive. They are more difficult to pronounce. And when used, they can lend an air

Table 4.1 Word Pairs

Perfectly good English	More impressive corporate-speak
Use	Utilize
Improve	Optimize
Fix	Solution (v)
Put into practice	Operationalize
Honest	Transparent

of importance, education, and even cryptic genius to the speaker. Here is a before and after comparison that illustrates the "power" of using better-version jargon. The first sentence uses clear language:

> Our company needs to improve how we get more productivity out of our employees, and we need to be honest with those employees about what we need from them.

While clear, it lacks the sizzle and pop that one would expect from a newly minted MBA. Let's "upgrade" it using better-version jargon:

> Cross-enterprise we must optimize how we utilize our FTEs, and as we solution for this we need to stress transparency so we can operationalize this successfully.

Wow! We just became management consultants. Send the bill.

All kidding aside, effective leaders skip the better version when choosing their words because they know that *what they have to say is meaningful on its own* and should not be dressed up or overloaded.

THE UNNECESSARY ADD-ON

Another example of inflation jargon is the "unnecessary add-on." This is simply a phrase or expression tacked on to the beginning or the end of a sentence. It serves little purpose aside from making the sentence more cumbersome, baffling, and yet seemingly more impressive-sounding.

In 2012 *Entrepreneur* published a list of the 10 most hated expressions in business. High on the list is the ever-present phrase, "At the end of the day. ..."[3] If you've ever sat in on a boardroom meeting, you've heard this expression before. Here are some recent shining examples of this unnecessary add-on in action:

"At the end of the day, it's all about the customer."

"At the end of the day, it just keeps coming back to our people."

"At the end of the day, we need to get this acquisition done."

You can understand why people have come to hate this useless phrase. Sadly, it is but one of many unnecessary add-ons that attach themselves, parasitically, to sentences that may have some measure of substance. Like any parasite, the unnecessary add-on does not kill its host, but merely drains and weakens it.

As leaders, we must always be watching to see if these linguistic parasites have fastened on to sentences of meaning and value. To assist you with this task, I have created a game called "Unnecessary Add-On Bingo," which you are free to use and reproduce for your own purposes in meetings, presentations, and other forums where unnecessary add-ons may be present (see Table 4.2).

Playing "Unnecessary Add-On Bingo"[4] is easy: bring it to your meetings or other corporate functions. Hold a pen in one hand and wait. When you hear one of the expressions on the card, put an X in that box. If you get five in a row, you win (though you may have, in a spiritual sense, lost). The winner's prize? You have earned the right to get up and walk out of the meeting with your dignity intact.

Leaders skip unnecessary add-ons for the simple reason that these words fail to add any meaning. They know that their ideas are what matter, and attaching additional language only diminishes the strength of those ideas.

Table 4.2   Unnecessary Add-On Bingo

At the end of the day…	…on a go-forward basis.	The bottom line is…	Net net…	To be honest with you…
To make a long story short…	Technically speaking…	I don't mean to offend you, but…	Having said that…	At this moment in time…
The reality is…	…but the future will tell	★	It's not rocket science…	If you really think about it…
Just sayin'…	You've probably already thought of this…	It's all about…	Let's net it out…	Strategically speaking…
The fact of the matter is…	To boil it down…	It is what it is…	It all adds up to…	With all due respect…

THE BAFFLING NOUN CLUSTER

Yet another example of inflationary language is the "baffling noun cluster." This is the linguistic equivalent of Dr. Frankenstein's monster. A noun cluster on its own "is a string of four or more words that normally function as nouns but don't mean anything."[5] A baffling noun cluster is a combination of disparate parts whose sum is terrifying to behold.

How is the baffling noun cluster created? Take this (very) short list of innocuous nouns that can be found in any typical corporate environment:

Team

Strategy

Plan

Priority

List

Timeline

Roadmap

Capital

Acquisition

Solution

Standing on their own, each of these nouns could be defined with (relative) ease; their meanings are, for the most part, easily understood. But now for the magic of the baffling noun cluster. Witness what can be created with the 10 nouns listed above:

Capital Priority Roadmap Solution;

Team Priority Plan Strategy;

Acquisition List Solution Roadmap.

Try it yourself! It's easy to create noun clusters! Watch this:

Team;

Acquisition Team;

Acquisition Team Strategy;

Acquisition Team Strategy Roadmap;

Acquisition Team Strategy Roadmap Solution;

Acquisition Team Strategy Roadmap Solution Priority.

As these examples illustrate, the beauty of the baffling noun cluster is that every noun you add exponentially decreases the clarity of what you are saying, while simultaneously increasing how "smart" you sound.

Here's what Marcia Riefer Johnston, author of *Word Up!*, has to say about noun clusters:

Sometimes called *noun stacks*, *noun strings*, or *noun compounds – noun piles*, anyone? – noun clusters can shut down your comprehension even if you understand each word. You may stop and reread. You may draw an incorrect conclusion. You may skip over the words. Or you may do the last thing the writer wanted you to do: move on to someone else's words.

To bust noun clusters when you write or edit, first get clear on what you want to say. If you don't know, ask; you can't bust a noun cluster until you understand what it means – and noun clusters notoriously obscure meaning.[6]

Leaders know that although noun clusters *sound impressive*, they should be avoided because they are not readily understood by audiences.

SUMMARY

The seemingly-better version. The unnecessary add-on. The baffling noun cluster. All three are examples of how language can be used to inflate the importance of otherwise mundane thinking. The chief, and very temporary, benefit of using this kind of inflationary jargon is to make speakers seem smarter than they are.

But there is a steep price to be paid for this: incomprehension. At best, audiences are impressed because they blame themselves for not being able to understand. More likely, they tune out because they don't understand what is being said. In either case, the speaker has failed to demonstrate leadership.

NOTES

1. "'Weird Al' Reopens Debate on Corporate Jargon," Public Affairs Council (October 2014), http://pac.org/news/comm/weird-al-reopens-debate-on-corporate-jargon.
2. Marcia Riefer Johnston, *Word Up! How To Write Powerful Sentences and Paragraphs* (Portland, OR: Northwest Brainstorms Publishing, 2012), 19.

3. Michael Sebastian, "The 10 Most Useless Buzzwords," *Entrepreneur* (December 20, 2012), http://www.entrepreneur.com/article/225310.

4. Credit for this concept must be given to a game called "Bullshit Bingo" that my friends and I faxed to each other early in my career when people still faxed things to each other. Sadly, while the fax machine may be on its last legs, the jargon that populated that bingo card lives on today.

5. Marcia Riefer Johnston, "What a (Noun) Cluster," Content Rules, http://www.contentrules.com/blog/noun-cluster/.

6. Ibid.

5

LACK-OF–CLARITY JARGON

'Twas brillig, and the slithy toves
Did gyre and gimble in the wabe:
All mimsy were the borogoves,
And the mome raths outgrabe.

"Beware the Jabberwock, my son!
The jaws that bite, the claws that catch!
Beware the Jubjub bird, and shun
The frumious Bandersnatch!"

He took his vorpal sword in hand;
Long time the manxome foe he sought —
So rested he by the Tumtum tree
And stood awhile in thought.

And, as in uffish thought he stood,
The Jabberwock, with eyes of flame,
Came whiffling through the tulgey wood,
And burbled as it came!

One, two! One, two! And through and through
The vorpal blade went snicker-snack!
He left it dead, and with its head
He went galumphing back.

"And hast thou slain the Jabberwock?
Come to my arms, my beamish boy!
O frabjous day! Callooh! Callay!"
He chortled in his joy.

'Twas brillig, and the slithy toves
Did gyre and gimble in the wabe:
All mimsy were the borogoves,
And the mome raths outgrabe.

—Lewis Carroll, "Jabberwocky"

If you have read Lewis Carroll's wonderful 1871 novel *Through the Looking Glass, and what Alice Found There,* you almost certainly remember the moment when Alice meets the White King and White Queen and finds a book that includes the nonsense poem "Jabberwocky." The brilliance of the poem is that it *sounds* like English, and holds true to English syntax and poetic structure, yet is riddled with nonsensical words that defy explanations. What is "Bandersnatch" or a "Jubjub bird"? What does it mean to "outgrabe" or to "burble"? What characteristics do we ascribe to the adjectives "frumious," "mimsy," or "uffish"?

Alice's take on the poem? "'It seems very pretty,' she said when she had finished it, 'but it's RATHER hard to understand!' (You see she didn't like to confess, ever to herself, that she couldn't make it out at all.) 'Somehow it seems to fill my head with ideas – only I don't exactly know what they are!'"

Alice's reaction to "Jabberwocky" is honest and revealing – the words are impressive and impenetrable all at once. Alice is reluctant, though, to admit – even to herself – that she cannot fully understand what she is hearing.

Carroll's book was published nearly 150 years ago, yet he was prescient in his foretelling of the rise of nonsense speak. Today's workplace environments are rife with speakers who spew jargon that sounds like English but is fundamentally meaningless. Some examples:

- The executive I mentioned in the introduction who confidently stated, "It's essential that we leverage Boston on a go-forward basis if we are going to grow AUM."
- A young project manager who was put on the spot about why his costs were over budget and who replied that "it is what it is; when we look at the quantum we see there are a lot of moving parts and we can't try to boil the ocean on this one while we revector."
- A silicon valley executive who, when asked about the possibility of layoffs due to poor results, said, "Well, I can't open the kimono too much on this one without aside from saying we've got our SWAT team on that as we focus on the possibility we have to pivot to increase our disruption and penetration."

In any of these situations we could imagine Alice, sitting in the audience, thinking to herself: "... it's RATHER hard to understand! ... Somehow it seems to fill my head with ideas – only I don't exactly know what they are!"

I refer to this type of jargon as "lack-of-clarity" jargon. Unlike assumption jargon (which actually has a meaning, only one that the speaker fails to define), lack-of-clarity jargon is a *substitute for meaning*. The speaker uses the words to replace clarity of thought. This is a greater sin for leaders than failing to define one's terminology. In fact, next to the kind of jargon that is used intentionally to baffle and mislead audiences (which we will examine more closely in the next chapter), this is the most ineffective and damaging kind of jargon that leaders can use.

LACK OF CLARITY ON THE JARGON SPECTRUM

Jargon that reflects a lack of clarity is on the far right of the jargon spectrum (see Figure 5.1) because it is, at best, ineffective and, at worst, highly damaging for those who wish to lead.

Figure 5.1 The Jargon Spectrum.

Why is this kind of jargon so dangerous for leaders? Leaders seek to inspire others to act; they achieve this by providing clear, powerful ideas that move others. Their language needs to reflect that clarity.

Yet, lack-of-clarity jargon is used as a substitute for clear thinking. It replaces the hard work of presenting clear arguments with a collection of terms that sound impressive but which, upon closer examination, are hollow.

Because so few people (like Alice) are willing to question those who use this kind of jargon, speakers may perceive it to be reaching their audiences when, in fact, it has the opposite effect. And when audiences do actually challenge speakers to define their terminology, they often expose the jargon as a flimsy cover over a lack of substance.

⌘

A SUBSTITUTE FOR THE HARD WORK OF THINKING

Clear thinking is hard work. It takes tremendous time and energy to hone and define an idea with the precision that audiences crave. In our era of email, Twitter, and Snapchat, the deep thinking required to reach this clarity can feel time-consuming and difficult.

But if you want to lead, undertaking this hard work is essential to your success. If you are going to ask others to take action, you must be able to put forth well-defined and compelling ideas worth acting upon. In some cases, these ideas are "visionary," big-picture thoughts – for example, a change in company strategy. In other instances, they are smaller-scale ideas, for example, showing employees how they can most effectively build business relationships. Yet, regardless of the scale of the idea, you must invest the time to achieve clarity of thought before seeking to inspire others (more on how actually to do this in Chapters 7, 8, and 9).

Using lack-of-clarity jargon allows speakers to circumvent this requirement and instead use words that *suggest* clarity lurks beneath what they are saying. Although few audiences will challenge speakers on their terminology, many – like Alice – may instinctively *know* that the words are meaningless.

Here's Darren Yaworsky, Vice President and Treasurer at Canadian Pacific Railway:

> Earlier in my career, [I remember an executive] who established a vision for the finance group to become a world class finance group. On the surface that's inspiring, but what does world class mean? What does world class mean in the context of the finance group that is specific to the company that I worked at, at that point in time? What does that specifically mean to the individuals? My first task was to define the vision.

Here's Anne Sado, President of George Brown College in Toronto, talking about some of the terminology in the world of education and why it lacks clarity:

> [The word] internationalization ... means different things to different people .... We are trying to internationalize our curriculum to achieve a number of goals, including offshore co-op placements or understanding cultural context in what we teach, given the diversity of our society. [The word] probably does mean 10 different things to any 10 different people that you might talk to about it. It's one of those very broad concepts, and sometimes I feel people like using it because it's seen as a popular trend or area of focus.
>
> Another fascinating one right now in our sector is differentiation. Well we are trying to figure that word out as well.

And here's Marcella Szel, Chair of the Board at Translink, talking about jargon that lacked substance during her career:

> I remember for a period of time the hot buzzword was, "Peel back the onion." Everybody was saying, "Well, look at this problem and let's just peel the onion back." I call that meaningless jargon.

These examples reflect the fact that such jargon will not inspire audiences, it will baffle them. Much as Lewis Carroll's "'Twas brillig, and the slithy toves/Did gyre and gimble in the wabe:/All mimsy were the borogoves,/And the mome raths outgrabe." Even when listeners do not question the meaning (due to seniority, or perceived lack of expertise), they may well pick up on the fact that there isn't much substance beneath the mask. And that can be dangerous – because masks can be removed.

❧

VULNERABLE TO EXPOSURE

When audiences do challenge speakers to define the jargon they are using, the results can be dire – for the speakers and their hopes of leading.

Here's how Geri Prior, Chief Financial Officer at the Insurance Corporate of British Columbia (ICBC), explains it:

> To me, it's always an indication of how well you understand the concept because for people that stay in that jargon world, sometimes when you dig down, they don't understand it as well as you think. So they are using it almost as a mask . . . . It's a cloak. . . .

After all, if speakers do not know what the words they are using mean, they will be unable to define them for others. When challenged, speakers are left with only two choices: admit their own lack of knowledge (as did the individual whom I asked to explain what "leverage Boston" meant) or go on the defensive by trying to explain their jargon with even more jargon.

I remember a coaching session I was having with Jeff, a young director in a Vancouver-based gas utility. Jeff was viewed as high potential, but his manager, the Vice President of Asset Management, often struggled to understand him. "Maybe he's just smarter than me," said the VP, "in fact, he probably is smarter than me. He's certainly better educated – Jeff has his MBA and I don't. But the fact is that I just can't understand him sometimes and neither can the executives here. And until he makes more sense it will hold him back."

In our first session, Jeff and I were working to prepare him for a major presentation to the utility's operating committee. The presentation was about capital investment in the company's aging infrastructure. Jeff did a dry run as I listened and counted the buzzwords: "blue sky it," "aligning," "re-visioning," "futuring," and, of course, a lot of "leveraging."

Five minutes in I interrupted Jeff and said, "Jeff, I have no idea what you are saying here. Can you explain it to me more clearly?"

"Sure, well aligning our asset management strategic framework …that's really about benchmarking things on a go-forward basis so we can hit the bogey.…"

I stopped him again and asked him to explain it to me as if I were a fifth grader. He paused, looked angry, and then sighed, deflated.

"Well, I guess I'm not exactly sure what to say. I know the operating committee is expecting big things of me and this is my chance to shine…so I want to show them that I'm up on the bleeding-edge thinking."

When Jeff realized his approach left him vulnerable, he took a step back and we started doing the hard work of figuring out what he wanted to say. Jeff had told me earlier he had a seven-year-old son, and so I got into character and asked him to explain the concept in plain language. Whenever I didn't understand something I told him, forcing him to get clear with the words he was using. I helped him by using an app on my phone that is a buzzer (it may qualify as the best 99 cents I ever spent). Whenever he used jargon I hit the buzzer. When Jeff realized how often I was buzzing him he started laughing. Two hours later, he had gotten to the point, and the result was a simple, yet powerful idea:

"Our infrastructure is aging faster than we thought, and we have to invest in it now or be stuck with a bigger bill tomorrow."

I had been able to "expose" Jeff's jargon as lacking in substance in the safety of our coaching session, giving him a chance to figure out what he really wanted to say. Informed leaders know they must do this hard work before speaking or risk similar exposure on high-stakes stages.

Two weeks later Jeff called me, excited to report that his presentation had been a success. He had only needed five minutes to present his case, and the operating committee asked him to build out his recommendations into a plan. Jeff had gotten some kudos from his VP as well. He didn't know it, but I knew then that Jeff was on his way not only to getting support for his idea but also to removing a barrier to his own advancement.

WORDS OF THE DAY

One of the easiest ways to get caught using "lack-of-clarity" jargon is to appropriate the "hot" terminology that is in circulation. Examples are everywhere.

On May 12, 2015, Verizon announced that it would acquire AOL Inc. In announcing the deal Tim Armstrong, AOL's Chairman and CEO, said:

> Verizon is a leader in mobile and OTT connected platforms, and the combination of Verizon and AOL creates a unique and scaled mobile and OTT media platform for creators, consumers and advertisers.[1]

What exactly is "a unique and scaled mobile and OTT platform"? While Mr Armstrong likely has clarity in his mind about what this term means . . . few listeners would.

Like fashion, language is ever-changing. Every year there are new buzzwords – like "unique and scaled mobile and OTT media platform," I suppose – that become part of the lexicon and, when used, signify that the speaker is up-to-date with current ideas and is follow-ing the "thought leaders" of the day. Using the term "transparency" in 1999 would have gotten you a weird look from audiences who might have thought you wanted an acetate sheet for an overhead projector; using transparency after the financial crash of 2008 would have put you in the "in" club. Talking about "disruption" in 1990 might have made audiences think you wanted to cause a scene, while using the term today is *de rigueur* for anyone in the tech industry.

Yet, leaders know that latching on to these "words of the day" is dan-gerous because those terms can too easily give the appearance of knowl-edge while discouraging the user from doing the hard work needed for precision.

While researching this book, I happened upon a clever concept pub-lished by *Fast Company* in 2015: a jargon "tournament." The idea was to "pit" hated terms against each other and to let readers vote on which was most offensive.

Ultimately, *Wired* would "crown" the most hated piece of jargon in business.

Here's *Fast Company*'s explanation of the game (see Figure 5.2):

We've gathered 32 of the most offensive examples of business jargon that's muddling communication in offices around the world, and all week we're letting you vote for the worst of the worst.

The "Final Four" was a premier list of awful jargon: "Synergy" (it's a noun! It's a verb! It's meaningless!), "Run Up The Flagpole" (or you could just ask people what they think...) and the eventual win-ner..."Opening the Kimono" (a great example of how jargon can make you sound like a porn commentator).

Fast Company's list is by no means exhaustive. Other loathed expres-sions include "strategizing," "empowering," "penetrating the market," "servicing the customer," and perhaps most awfully, "Drinking the Kool-Aid." For those of you who don't know, this term is a euphemism for "someone who has a cult-like level of commitment and devotion to our cause." The origin of this expression? In November 1978 over 900 members of Jim Jones's Peoples Temple cult committed suicide

Figure 5.2   The Jargon Matchup Game.

Source: Fast Company, Vote for the Worst Business Jargon of All Time (http://www.fastcompany.com/3049222/vote-for-the-worst-business-jargon-of-all-time).

by drinking a Kool-Aid-like drink laced with cyanide.[3] That this tragic event is now used as a positive affirmation of commitment to a company is indicative of the horrors of business jargon.

We can't know what the next words of the day will be – only that they will exist. Tempting though it may be to gain admittance to the "thought leader" club by appropriating them, resist the urge. Leaders know that powerful, clear thinking is best expressed with words that are free from jargon and instead convey the essence of the idea.

SUMMARY

Developing clear, compelling ideas is hard work – otherwise everyone would create them. In many instances, speakers lack the time and inclination to undertake this hard work and achieve a clarity of thought. Instead, they use jargon as a substitute, which often goes unchallenged by audiences who may ascribe more expertise to the speaker than is warranted.

Yet, such language leaves the speaker vulnerable to exposure and, more importantly, the speaker fails to inspire others to act. That is why effective leaders listen and reject "lack-of-clarity" jargon and choose powerful, clear words that convey the substance of the ideas they have worked so hard to develop.

NOTES

1. http://www.prnewswire.com/news-releases/verizon-to-acquire-aol-300081541.html.
2. https://en.wikipedia.org/wiki/Drinking_the_Kool-Aid.
3. http://www.forbes.com/business-jargon/.

6

OBFUSCATION JARGON

If you know what obfuscation means, I commend you. If you don't, you would be well within your rights to ask why a book about the language of leadership would contain a chapter titled with a rarely used word that essentially means *to conceal*. Specifically, *Merriam-Webster's* definition of the verb *obfuscate* is:

1. To make obscure <*obfuscate* the issue>;
2. To be evasive, unclear, or confusing.

The reason obfuscation is included in the title of the chapter is that far too often jargon is used by speakers for the purpose of obscuring or concealing realities from audiences. Far too often such jargon is purposefully used to confuse, bewilder, *and* stupefy audiences in order to prevent the reactions they would have if they understood the meaning of the terms being used.

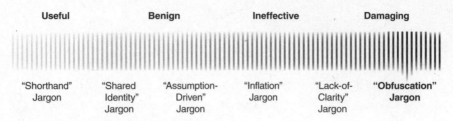

Figure 6.1 The Jargon Spectrum.

OBFUSCATION ON THE JARGON SPECTRUM

Language that is meant to intentionally baffle or conceal sits squarely on the far right (negative) side of the Jargon Spectrum (see Figure 6.1). Such language is not reflective of leadership because it creates barriers between speakers and their listeners.

Sometimes obfuscation is used unconsciously, and other times intentionally. Regardless of the reason for its use, it should be avoided at all costs. The bottom line: leaders should not hide behind jargon. Here's what Steve Reid, board member at Silver Standard and Eldorado Gold, and the former Chief Operating Officer at Goldcorp, told me:

> I worked for a COO in a multi-national company who was the most inspiring or influential leader [in my career]. There was no ambiguity about what he was saying. He was always clear. He came across very genuinely and I can't think of him hiding behind jargon in any point in time. There was just absolute clarity.

On the surface, it seems obvious that leaders should be direct and not conceal their meaning by using "bafflegab" or other jargon. Yet, time and again well-intentioned speakers fall into this trap and replace clarity with obfuscation. Why do they do this?

Obfuscation to Conceal Uncomfortable Truths

The most common reason speakers use language to hide their meaning is their own discomfort with what they have to say. In the workplace, nothing makes people more anxious or uncomfortable than the thought of losing their job – and for managers, the thought of having to tell employees that they are losing their jobs. That's why it is unsurprising how much language has been created to say "You're fired" or "You can no longer work here" without actually saying it. Consider the following short list of alternative words that are often used:

Exiting

Packaging

Terminating

Severing

Rightsizing

Restructuring

Downsizing

Decruiting

And my personal "favorite" –

Releasing to the marketplace.

This language exists and is used because it allows managers to depersonalize the very difficult and sometimes traumatic reality that they are ending an employee's employment. Instead of saying, "I am telling you your job is over and you cannot come to work Monday," they can say, "The company is in the midst of an enterprise rightsizing that necessitates us to align FTEs with boxes and the assessment of your position unfortunately found we have to seek efficiencies that will eliminate your role."

Much clearer, isn't it?

Yet this isn't the only topic where discomfort on the part of the speaker (or the organization) leads to this linguistic concealment.

Consider the world of education. Here's what Emily Mather, a high school teacher (who also happens to be my wife), says:

> There is no question this kind of language exists in report cards and parent–teacher interviews when it comes to talking about child behavior in class. Teachers generally have no problem giving feedback on performance and achievement, and recommending solutions like tutors or extra help. But teachers are often uncomfortable giving feedback on behavior when the child's misbehaving affects the whole class.
>
> So teachers who want to address behavioral issues often resort to "teacher-speak." No parent wants to hear that their child is the worst behaved in class or having a negative impact on the learning of other children. Or that they are distracting the teacher constantly.
>
> So we write "his behavior takes away from his learning" instead of saying "he isn't doing any of his work in class." We write "he is more interested in the work of other students than his own" instead of saying "he is always bothering other kids instead of paying attention to his own work." We write, "he relies too heavily on teacher for direction," instead of "your child never thinks for himself." Or a classic one – they "do not display age-appropriate behavior" is teacher-speak for "your child is immature."
>
> We do this because we are uncomfortable with telling parents about behavioral and attention issues. So we resort to teacher-speak to start the dialogue without being offensive. But the ramification is that parents are confused and many never find out the reality, which doesn't help the parent, the teacher, or the student.

OBFUSCATION CAN BE USED TO AVOID OR DEFER CONFLICT

Another reason speakers use language that obfuscates is to avoid conflict. Over and over in my interviews, senior leaders shared stories with me of how they heard – and used – language that was meant to baffle an audience as a means of avoiding confrontation.

Bruno Sperduti is the Executive Vice President of Rental Management at FirstService Residential; previously, he held the role of Chief

Information Officer for the company from 2007 to 2014. He shared with me a story of when he held the CIO role and had the mandate to bring a common set of software offerings to the many companies that had been acquired under the national company banner, but which had all retained their own unique IT solutions. It was the right move for the business – but it also meant asking the founders and CEOs of the acquired companies to put aside what was best for them individually and embrace a solution that was best for the company nationally.

Bruno describes how he and his team spoke to these leaders about what they proposed:

> We would talk a lot about an enterprise application, [which we also called] nationalization. These terms were meant to describe a solution that applied to all companies, including theirs. We knew it was jargon – enterprise was a big term for us. By enterprise, we meant one platform, but the real message was, you don't have a choice but to use it.

I asked Bruno whether terms like "enterprise" and "nationalization" were clearly understood to mean "you will get the solution that is best for our company but not for your individual business." He told me:

> Initially we didn't use the term – we were very clear and spelled out strategy. But then we deferred to the cooler word: "enterprise" and, in our minds, we still felt that it would help everybody to go along with it without us having high-conflict conversations or those where we would get a lot of questions.

When I asked Bruno how this approach worked out, he was clear it wasn't successful beyond the short-term gain of avoiding conflict:

> It didn't work very well. Why? Because it didn't create the type of collaboration between our corporate office and the regional offices to really agree on how this strategy was to work. And every time we used the jargon, it just reinforced the need to continue using it more. And the result was [that] I don't think we pulled everybody else along with us.

Bruno's story is quite typical because it takes an incredible amount of time and energy to win people over to your point of view – and even the most impassioned leaders will be unable to win *everyone* they need over to their side. So it can be tempting to bypass the conflict that often accompanies persuasion and conceal what is happening by using obfuscating language. Yet, as Bruno described, the price you pay is a lack of long-term buy-in, or worse, a loss of trust when audiences realize what is happening.

OBFUSCATION CAN BE USED TO CONFUSE AND MISLEAD

While most obfuscation is born of discomfort or the desire to avoid conflict, in some cases there are more nefarious motives. In some instances, speakers intentionally choose language that will allow them to conceal unpleasant realities from their audiences so that they ask no questions and accept less-than-desirable outcomes.

In his book, *Becoming a Critical Thinker*, Robert Todd Carroll explains:

> Jargon can also be used to create technical sounding euphemisms that try to hide ugly realities or make bad or indifferent things seem good or fantastic. Such jargon can have the effect of deceiving us about things that are dangerous, harmful, or wasteful.

He then goes on to give numerous examples, the most shocking of which has to be this one:

> In a footnote in the National Airlines' annual report for 1978, National explained that revenues of $1.7 million came from "the involuntary conversion of a 727." Three of the fifty-two people aboard the involuntarily converted airplane were killed in the crash. What stockholder wants to be reminded that profits were made from an after-tax insurance benefit from the accident?[1]

National Airlines had to report on the financial costs of the crash – yet wanted to use language that would preclude any questions about the crash. The company's choice of words is shocking: involuntary conversion. This is a prime example of obfuscation used intentionally and with no sense of moral responsibility.

I saw another example of this kind of intentional obfuscation when I was reading one of my favorite authors, Michael Lewis, the author of *Liar's Poker*. Lewis has long written about the behavior of bankers and financiers whose interests do not align with those of their clients. In his book, *Boomerang*, he writes about the negative consequences of cheap credit on countries like Ireland, Iceland, and Germany. In his chapter on Germany, he writes about "a bank called IKB, who were up to something new." Lewis goes on to describe how IKB was created:

> [It was] in effect, a bank…[but] [t]hey didn't call it a bank. If they had called it a bank, people might have asked why it was not regulated. They called it a "conduit," a word that had the advantage that no one understood what it meant.[2]

What's in a name? By calling itself a conduit this bank avoided regulation. Then it used this non-regulated status to pursue all sorts of ill-advised transactions that had dire consequences. This kind of intentional obfuscation has no place in the language of leadership. It aims to confuse and conceal rather than to influence and inspire. It results in resentment and can cause a backlash when audiences realize what is happening. And it does not serve the interests of leaders who wish to inspire a genuine following in their audiences.

SOMETIMES OBFUSCATION IS UNINTENTIONAL

Some speakers who use jargon may be perceived to be using language to obfuscate, even when they may not have intended to do so. This can occur when a speaker uses ill-defined buzzwords or jargon that various listeners can and do interpret differently.

In my interview with Martha Fell, a former Executive Director at one of Canada's five largest financial institutions, and the former CEO of Women in Capital Markets, she told me about an expression she heard frequently by speakers who used it in a positive way. It was a word she came to dislike:

> [I struggle with the word] meritocracy. A lot of firms say they support a meritocratic environment and that if you work really hard and produce excellent results you will be compensated and recognized accordingly. Unfortunately, I think most companies fail to execute their plan to pay and recognize people fairly because it is so subjective and at management's discretion.
>
> So, if a manager says, "I believe in meritocracy," in a town hall meeting and goes on about how they are going to allocate compensation and bonuses, and whatnot, for some people it sounds disingenuous because they don't believe that in fact they are going to be compensated or they are going to be recognized. And therefore many of them will end up asking for recognition or more pay.
>
> The frustration stems from the fact that even though the industry espouses a meritocracy, those who don't ask but rather expect to be paid accordingly, many – and women in particular – have experienced disappointment, myself included. The manager's subjectivity involved in setting salaries, determining raises or bonuses results in these discrepancies in pay, and made the word a point of frustration, especially for women.

In this instance, the obfuscation was likely unintentional. The speakers were not *trying* to paper over the lack of advancement that women were experiencing in investment banking. But, as Martha points out, the fact that their language didn't fit with reality meant the speakers who used the term "meritocracy" were viewed by many in the audience as deceitful.

SUMMARY

Why do speakers use language that intentionally clouds and confuses? Often they do so because they are uncomfortable with the realities they are describing or because they wish to pre-empt conflict. In other instances, obfuscation is intentional – driven by a desire to limit understanding. Whatever the reason, this kind of jargon has no place in the language of leaders.

NOTES

1. Robert Todd Carroll, *Becoming a Critical Thinker*, Chapter 2, http://skepdic.com/refuge/ctlessons/ch2.pdf.
2. Michael Lewis, *Boomerang: Travels in the New Third World* (New York: W.W. Norton, 2012), 158.

Part II

Use the Language of Leadership

Introduction to Part II: Use the Language of Leadership

I say to you today, my friends, so even though we face the difficulties of today and tomorrow, I still have a dream. It is a dream deeply rooted in the American dream.

I have a dream that one day this nation will rise up and live out the true meaning of its creed: "We hold these truths to be self-evident; that all men are created equal."

I have a dream that one day on the red hills of Georgia the sons of former slaves and the sons of former slave owners will be able to sit down together at the table of brotherhood.

I have a dream that one day even the state of Mississippi, a state sweltering with the heat of injustice, sweltering with the heat of oppression, will be transformed into an oasis of freedom and justice.

I have a dream that my four little children will one day live in a nation where they will not be judged by the color of their skin but by the content of their character.

I have a dream today!

Martin Luther King Jr., August 28, 1963

The words of Dr King inspired hundreds of thousands of Americans to believe that civil rights, equality, and justice were all possible. While not fully realized, the tremendous progress made in the United States – and the world – since that day are powerful reminders of what leaders can inspire others to achieve.

Dr King's words serve as a powerful reminder that language can be invigorating and memorable. His use of rhetorical devices such as repetition, parallel structure, antithesis, and metaphor (all explained in detail in Chapter 20) enabled his audience to hear and retain his ideas. His words are an outstanding example of the language of leadership. But the language of leadership isn't just for civil rights leaders, or CEOs, or motivational speakers.

If you are a senior project manager in an aerospace company who needs to motivate your team to deliver on time and on budget – you need to use the language of leadership.

If you are a director of internal audit at a telecommunications company who needs to have management take seriously the problems you have found, you need to use the language of leadership.

If you are a hospital administrator who wants physicians to embrace more consistent hand-washing practices – you need to use the language of leadership.

If you are a vice president of marketing at an internet start-up where engineers make all the decisions and your marketing ideas are dismissed as "fluff" – you need to use the language of leadership.

If you are a Grades 7–8 special needs teacher who wants her school to adopt new methods to help children with dyslexia – you need to use the language of leadership.

No matter what organization you are in or what role you hold, if you want to inspire change, you must make the choice to speak as a leader and to express your ideas using the language of leadership.

In Part I of this book you learned how leaders think about jargon — and why they almost always avoid it. In Part II you will learn not just why jargon rarely inspires but, more importantly, *what to say instead* so you will reach your listeners and move them to action. In short, you will learn to use the language of leadership.

WHAT IS THE LANGUAGE OF LEADERSHIP?

Let's go back to our definition of a leader:

> *A leader is someone who inspires others to act.*

Remember — leaders earn the right to be heard. They create followers through the clarity and power of their ideas, rather than through coercion or manipulation. They recognize that this inspirational approach is the only way to create long-term commitment in those whom they wish to reach.

Think of the language of leadership as a tool for leaders — one that enables them to articulate and convey the ideas they want others to hear and act upon. This brings us to our next definition:

> *The language of leadership refers to the words used to convey ideas that inspire others.*

You should choose your words consciously, carefully, and deliberately. In doing so, you will increase not only the chance that you will inspire your listeners but also your own confidence in your ability to convey your message clearly.

HOW TO USE THE LANGUAGE OF LEADERSHIP

In Part II of this book you will learn how to use the language of leadership. But you cannot achieve this simply by selecting "inspiring" and "authentic" words from a list. You cannot copy Steve Jobs's or Martin Luther King Jr.'s rhetoric. What you will learn is that there are three

| 1. Adopt the leader's mindset | 2. Script yourself as a leader | 3. Use the language of leadership |

Figure II.1   Three Steps to Speaking Like a Leader.

steps you must follow to speak like a leader and to use words that will energize others (see Figure II.1).

First, you must adopt the leader's mindset. In Part I of this book we saw how looking at jargon through the lens of leadership clarified its uses and abuses. Now we will explore how you can look at what you want to say through the same lens. You will learn that the starting point for inspirational communication lies in the mindset you bring to your interactions. In Chapter 7 you will learn how to think about your vision, define your convictions, and develop the courage to challenge others.

Second, you must script yourself as a leader. Once you have adopted the leader's mindset and decided what ideas you are passionate about, you must organize your thinking. In Chapter 8 you will learn how to "script" yourself as a leader by focusing your thinking around a clear message and supporting structure. Think of a script not as something you actually write down (though in some instances you may) but as well-organized thinking you carry around in your head, ready to share with your audience.

Third, you must use the language of leadership. Once you know what your script is, you must articulate it using language that showcases your leadership and inspires others to act upon it. In Chapters 10 to 20 you will learn how to do this, by making your language audience-centric, personal, authentic, confident, direct, and concise, while also drawing on the power of rhetoric.

In reading these steps your reaction may be, "I do many of these things already!" I'm sure you are thinking about leadership communication, delivering clear messages, and using inspiring words. Many of the clients we work with at The Humphrey Group come to us communicating in these ways as well; that is why they have upper-level positions as executives and managers.

Yet, few of our clients are able *consistently* and *repeatedly* to communicate in a way that inspires action. They may have some audiences with whom they excel at influencing while they struggle to connect with others. They may have moments of brilliance and then, because they aren't sure what made them so effective, later wonder "why can't I always be that brilliant?"

The most effective leaders understand that leadership communication is a skill you develop and one you apply with conscious intention. Doing so allows you to adapt to any audience while staying true to yourself.

As your self-awareness improves, you will learn how to make continual adjustments. I remember taking a great ski lesson in Whistler, British Columbia. The instructor taught me new ways to turn and edge on very steep terrain. As the lesson went on he provided assessments of what I was doing right and wrong. The result was that I was better able to evaluate my technique each time I skied. The same principle applies to leadership communication – when you understand the skills required to influence and inspire, you will also be able to self-assess and understand what you did right or wrong.

The key is to practice a repeatable methodology, and that approach is the three-step process of mindset, scripting, and language.

REPEATABLE COMMUNICATION METHODOLOGY

This three-part process is at the heart of the intellectual capital that my firm, The Humphrey Group, has used to help leaders communicate inspirationally for over 25 years. We call it our Leadership Model®, and with a fourth component (projecting a leader's presence), it serves as a repeatable methodology that you can use to speak as a leader in all interactions.

If you have read *Speaking as a Leader*, written by our founder Judith Humphrey, this framework will be familiar to you. What is different in this book is the depth with which we will examine the third com-ponent – language. While I dedicate a chapter to mindset and script, if you are keen to explore these topics in greater detail I encourage you to pick up *Speaking as a Leader*, which examines those areas in still greater detail.

Summary

In short, the key is to practice the three-step methodology of mindset, scripting and language. The ensuing chapters explore these topics. Let us now turn to the first step in the process of learning how to speak as a leader – mindset.

7

ADOPT THE LEADER'S MINDSET

Before I tell you what the language of leadership is, we need to step back a bit. The words leaders choose to use are simply the final articulation of the ideas and convictions they have defined and want to share with others.

Think of it this way: if you are going to build a house, you will need tools. But before you can decide which tools to buy, you first need to think about whom the house is for and what your vision for the house is. Once you've defined those two things, you can create a construction plan. Only then should you buy your tools.

The words you will use are like those tools. Choosing words too soon is pointless. That's why people decry those who "just open their mouths and start speaking" or who "seem to talk a lot but say very little." We value substance and precision in those we listen to.

| 1. Adopt the leader's mindset | 2. Script yourself as a leader | 3. Use the language of leadership |

Figure 7.1 Three Steps to Thinking Like a Leader.

That's why the most inspirational leaders get their thinking clear first; once they have that clarity of thought they are well-positioned to choose the words that will most effectively convey their ideas.

BEFORE YOU THINK ABOUT LANGUAGE, ADOPT THE LEADER'S MINDSET

Getting your thinking clear starts with adopting the right mindset (step 1 in the three-step process pictured in Figure 7.1). You are reading this book because you want to influence, motivate, and inspire others – that is why you must adopt a leader's mindset. At The Humphrey Group, we believe adopting such a mindset is a deliberate and conscious act.

The leader's mindset will help you think consciously about using communication as a vehicle for leadership. It is made up of six guiding principles, which collectively provide the foundation for speaking as a leader. These principles are as follows:

> **Principle One: Begin with vision.** All leaders have vision. Your vision must be an elevated reality that you want others to believe in. You must define the vision as a possibility that others can embrace or aspire to fulfill. Yet it must be concrete enough that people can grasp it as something clear and achievable.
>
> As Susan Uchida, Vice President of Learning at the Royal Bank of Canada, told me:

> When it comes to communication, the leader's role, I believe, is to be able to really articulate what your vision is and to help people understand what their part is in that.

Having this vision and infusing it in all your communication allows you to elevate your language from the merely functional to the language of leadership.

Principle Two: Define your own convictions. You must have convictions about your vision and the possibilities it represents. You must have convictions about the messages you deliver, which will, in turn, allow you to choose language that reflects your leadership. Conviction, as defined by *Merriam-Webster's Dictionary*, means "a strong persuasion or belief" and "the state of being convinced."

Developing these strong beliefs will free you to speak not only about what you know but also about what you believe. Your convictions will allow you to develop strong, deeply felt messages for each audience you speak to. They will encourage you to use powerful, passionate language; the language of belief rather than fact. They will encourage you to see that audiences are yearning for something to believe in, something to set their course by. And they will encourage you to see every occasion as a stage for your leadership.

When you speak from a place of conviction, your language becomes personal, authentic, and powerful. You will be able to use words that are meaningful to you and that express your commitment to your ideas.

Principle Three: Move from information to inspiration. The number one reason speakers fail to inspire their audiences is that they focus on conveying information rather than ideas.

This is not surprising; delivering information provides a safe haven. Who can quibble with the facts? Yet, audiences are drowning in information and are looking instead for clarity of thought. This informational approach also explains why so much language is dull, jargon-laden, or simply uninspiring. Information itself lacks the ability to move us and to transform our beliefs.

Leadership is not based on transferring information; it is based on transforming people. Leaders must move from an informational mode of speaking to an inspirational mode if they wish to engage and move others. Inspiration is the realm of true leadership, and any leader can achieve it. Inspiration, which comes from the words "into" and "breathe," means to instill in others the life, energy, and passion that are within you. To inspire requires you to speak with a deeply felt message, bring that message forward, and convince others of it. You can inspire others whether you are speaking about your company's business plan, your commitment to quality, or your excitement about merging two employee groups.

As Dane Jensen, CEO of Performance Coaching, told me:

Information doesn't do it for people...if information changed people, nobody would smoke, nobody would eat junk food, and everybody would workout. But [despite the availability of] information...people don't analyze and then act – people feel, and respond to that feeling. They have some emotion and that's what motivates people to act.

When you move away from this informational approach and choose instead to share your beliefs and convictions, you will find yourself using language that energizes your audiences. You will strip away and eliminate any jargon and complexity that impedes your ability to reach the hearts and minds of others.

Principle Four: Be courageous. History shows that any great leader faces the challenge of delivering messages that may not be well received. Martin Luther King Jr., John F. Kennedy, Margaret Thatcher, and Nelson Mandela were among the greatest orators of all time because they had the courage to express their convictions.

All leaders must grapple with the challenge of bringing forward their messages even in situations where they may encounter opposition. As organizations experience unprecedented change, more and more messages may require courage – the courage to tell people they may not have jobs; the courage to present a new vision when staff members have become comfortable with the old; the courage to acknowledge the need for a change in strategy. Think of Steve Jobs, who, upon his return to Apple in 1997, had the courage to say that the company had to stop pursuing most of its products and focus instead on four offerings.

You may not be faced with turning a company like Apple around. You may not be called upon to lead in tumultuous times. But if you intend to lead, you must be ready to deliver ideas that challenge your listeners to adopt new approaches. That boldness will demonstrate your refusal to become complacent, even on days when it might seem easier to just "coast." This is the everyday courage that is required to ensure that you inject your passion and vision into every meeting, email, and extemporaneous conversation.

Approaching communication with this courageous mindset will also shape the kind of language you choose. You will be more direct because you will welcome the chance to challenge views respectfully. You will eliminate "mincing modifiers" or "hedging" language that may undermine the strength of your ideas. And you will use powerful rhetorical devices such as repetition, metaphor, and rhetorical questions to bring your ideas to life.

Principle Five: Make it an everyday process. Leading takes place not only at the podium, but also in board rooms and meeting rooms, at town halls and on phone calls. It is the everyday speaking in elevators and on conference calls that represents the essence of leadership. Informal events are increasingly the default moments and opportunities for persuasion, for winning over employees, customers, and senior management.

When you think about leading in every interaction, you will not reserve the language of leadership for "command performances" like town halls but will instead use inspiring words in all situations. Your language will reflect your day-in-and-day-out commitment to sharing ideas that move audiences.

Principle Six: Be audience-centric. Many leaders don't ask themselves, "Why should my audience listen to me?" Instead, they focus on the content and information they want to share with their listeners.

To speak as a leader means you must engage your audience by showing them what's in it for them. Your audience must be uppermost in your mind even before you enter the room. A true leader asks, "What does my audience need from me?" "How can I move them?" "What message do I want them to take away and act upon?" This motivational intention shapes everything a speaker does from choosing a venue, to defining the topic, to developing the message, to carefully building a case for that point of view, to delivering with passion to evoke that same level of commitment in the audience.

This ability to understand an audience and only speak once that understanding is established distinguishes leaders. Here's Phillip Smith, Chief Financial Officer of Scotiabank's investment banking arm, Global Banking and Markets, discussing the skills shown by successful leaders:

> They really think before they speak. They don't speak, they don't dominate a conversation even though they are leaders [and more senior than others]. They always listen as much as they talk . . . they have listened to everyone ahead of time and are able to then cut through everything and say, "Look, here is where we are."

Audience-centered speaking is tough. But leaders need followers, and when you speak in a way that reaches the hearts and minds of an audience creates followers. This intention should produce humility in the speaker, and a sense in each member of the audience that the speaker cares about them and depends upon their commitment.

When you approach your communication through the lens of your audience, you will more readily choose language that resonates with your listeners. You will be able to use or reject jargon because of how it serves that particular audience, and you will express your ideas using words that resonate with them.

USING THE LEADER'S MINDSET IS A SKILL

Approaching all interactions as opportunities to lead is a learned skill. While every conversation, presentation, meeting, or Q&A scenario is different, there are common elements that leaders can learn to identify that will allow them to find the opportunity to influence the thinking of their audiences.

The key to developing this skill is commitment. You must commit to the process of analyzing every audience to determine what their beliefs and perspectives are and how you would like to move them. You must commit to the process of defining your own vision and convictions so you can share them with your audiences. You must commit to having the courage to present ideas that may be challenged.

Here's Jay Rosenzweig, President and CEO of Rosenzweig & Company, an international executive search firm, on the importance of commitment:

> I honestly feel that communication skills are by far the most important skills required to advance to the top of an organization. There's nothing that comes close second. Nothing.

> I think if someone wants to become a true leader, they need to work very hard on honing and perfecting their communication skills. I don't think there's anybody in the world who was simply born with perfect communication skills. It's an ongoing effort to develop them. Just like exercise, it needs to be a lifelong pursuit and there is always room to improve.

❧

SUMMARY

To sum up, the first step in developing your leadership communication skills is adopting a leader's mindset. It means approaching all your communication not just as a chance to convey information but as an opportunity to inspire action. It means developing clarity about what you believe in, and having the courage to challenge others to embrace those beliefs. It means taking the time to think about whom you wish to inspire, and then treating every conversation, every meeting, and every presentation as an opportunity to move them to action.

As you begin to use this new mental "muscle," you will find that you build "muscle memory" and the process of thinking as a leader will become second nature to you.

8

SCRIPT YOURSELF
AS A LEADER

Shakespeare once said, "All the world's a stage." He could have been talking about the corporate world, where you are always on stage – whether you like it or not! And like the actors who rehearse their lines and take the stage in *Hamlet,* you too are playing a part, complete with scripts of your own.

No actor would go on stage without learning their lines, and no leader worth their salt shows up at a meeting or at a Q&A without knowing their scripts. Although leaders are not usually handed written scripts (that is, unless they have full-time speech writers), the most effective individuals organize their thinking so they can inspire listeners when they do speak.

In the last chapter we examined how to develop a leader's mindset. In this chapter we look at the next step in speaking as a leader – organizing what you wish to say to others. This is a crucial step and requires hard work. If you want your audience to hear and act upon your ideas, they must be well thought out and compelling not only to your listeners but also to you.

1. Adopt the leader's mindset	2. Script yourself as a leader	3. Use the language of leadership

Figure 8.1 Three Steps to Thinking Like a Leader.

The most effective way to organize your thoughts is by scripting yourself (Figure 8.1).

What is a script? It is a well-defined set of ideas that you can articulate to others. Leaders are always scripting themselves. They know that in some instances – formal presentations, town halls, investor calls – they will have the time to prepare their scripts in advance. But they also know that in the majority of cases – informal conversations, chance meetings with customers, unexpected phone calls – they will not, and will only be able to speak as leaders if they have already done the hard work of getting their thinking clear in advance.

That's why the most effective leaders carry around a collection of "scripts" in their heads, and are ready for the various communication opportunities that inevitably come their way. They then adapt these scripts for a particular audience and are able to deliver them with authenticity and conviction.

Once you script yourself, you will find choosing the right words, that is, speaking in the "language of leadership," is much easier.

SCRIPTING YOURSELF AS A LEADER IS A SKILL YOU MUST DEVELOP

For over 25 years, our clients have told us that learning to script themselves is the most valuable skill we teach. Like any skill, it takes time and practice to build the mental muscle memory that makes it second nature. Here's Martha Fell on how learning to script herself became part of her routine:

> When I had to write speeches as the CEO of Women in Capital Markets, when I had to write sponsorship pitches for WCM, I would script myself – and focus my efforts on the opening (my grabber). Getting this

part right meant I could start powerfully, connecting with the audience the right way and getting them excited about my talk. I would write and revise it many times until I was satisfied with it.

I've even found myself scripting my emails – and again focusing my energy on the openings. This has become habitual for me and has increased the effectiveness [of my communication].

Here's Serge Roussel, Vice President of Finance at Pfizer, on the importance of scripting:

> You need to be clear in your mind . . . . If you don't get [clear], how can you expect others to understand and get it right?

When you see speakers who are "naturals," remember that they have worked unnaturally hard to achieve that level of proficiency. Martin Luther King Jr. was rewriting his "I Have a Dream" speech the morning it was delivered.[1] John F. Kennedy was intimately involved in the preparation of his speeches. Steve Jobs rehearsed product introductions meticulously so he could project an air of casual precision. While you may never need to speak to 1,000 people, if you want to lead and inspire others, you must develop a level of expertise in organizing and delivering your thinking.

GET YOUR THINKING CLEAR WITH THE LEADER'S SCRIPT

Scripting yourself as a leader means more than writing down what you intend to say – it means getting clarity about the message you wish to convey to your audience and ensuring that everything you say supports that message.

To help our clients script themselves as leaders, our company created a simple, yet powerful tool called the Leader's Script® (see Figure 8.2).

You can download an electronic version of this script from our website (www.thehumphreygroup.com). While this book's focus on language makes it impractical to go into depth about the Leader's Script®,

The Leader's Script®

Grabber: _____

Subject: _____

Message: _____

Structural
Statement: _____

Point One: _____

Point Two: _____

Point Three: _____

Restated
Message: _____

Call to Action: _____

Figure 8.2 The Leader's Script®.

I do want to examine the three most critical elements of this template: the subject, the message, and the call to action.

HAVE A CLEAR SUBJECT

The subject is a single sentence that defines for your audience what you want to talk about. An effective subject sets parameters of what will and will not be discussed; it helps the audience focus on your topic. It sets the stage for your message. Here are some examples of both weak and strong subject sentences:

Weak (too general): "I thought I could tell you a few things about this new product we're offering."

Strong: "In this presentation I would like to discuss the timing of the new product rollout and who will be accountable for each step."

Weak (overly focused, too negative): "We are meeting to go over the mistakes you have made."

Strong: "We are meeting to discuss creating a plan to help you get back to being a high performer."

Every time you speak you should have a clear subject. The language used to convey your subject will determine its effectiveness. In the first example the subject is a tentative "I thought" and an overly general "tell you a few things." The second example uses negative, punitive language, "...to go over the mistakes you have made," and would likely polarize the discussion before it started.

Yet, even an effective subject written in the language of leadership is not meant to inspire – its sole role is to define the topic for the audience. The inspiration comes in your message.

HAVE A LEADERSHIP MESSAGE

The most important component in the Leader's Script is the message. Every effective script has a *single* overall message. Why one message? Because it allows your audience – and you – to focus on a single powerful idea. Here's Dane Jensen, CEO of Performance Coaching, talking about the importance of having a single message:

[When I took over as CEO and would] go out and talk about what we do as an organization…I would make sure that there was something for everybody in what I was laying out. I would go through the six or seven programs that we offer.

Inevitably, when you start talking about that many different things, people start to get confused…. As you're starting to walk through them, you can imagine [that] for somebody who isn't living this every single day, [they will] start to get pretty confused about halfway through.

I've certainly found it is dramatically more effective to go into those types of conversations and say [to the audience], "I want to talk about the one thing that I think is going to be really relevant for [all of] you and we're going to focus on this one thing."

As Dane points out, having too many messages (or too many subjects) causes an audience to lose focus and interest. Leaders know that having a single message gives their communication clarity. They go into an interaction knowing exactly what idea they want the audience to hear and do not need to rely on ambiguous jargon to fill in the blanks.

Here are five key steps to ensure your message achieves this purpose:

- **It must be engaging:** If the audience isn't interested in or challenged by your message, it's an ineffective message. Too many corporate messages (e.g., "our best assets walk in the door every day") look superficially good but fail to engage and are viewed as little more than platitudes.

- **It must be positive:** As we will see in Chapter 16, leaders use language that is positive; they know that negatives create fear and that sustained support is possible only through positive thinking. Construct your message accordingly.

- **It must be something you believe in:** If you aren't inspired by your own message, why would anyone else be? Don't just parrot corporate slogans – make the argument your own.

- **It must fit with your organization's outlook:** No one ever wins followers by throwing their company under the bus. Be sure your message supports corporate goals and positions you as a change agent rather than as a griper.

- **It must square with the facts:** There had better be substance behind your message, or it may be one of the last ones your audience deigns to listen to.

Here are three examples of weak and strong messages:

Example 1

> **Weak (lacking personal commitment):** "The company's new strategy is designed to enable us to expand into the European retail market."

Strong: "I firmly believe that our new strategy will enable us to expand into the European retail market."

Example 2

Weak (negative, overly long): "You aren't really making this easy on us – we're supposed to be partners but you keep driving our pricing down – we'll do it if that's what it takes."

Strong: "We want to stress that this partnership is important to us – and we are willing to compromise on pricing to cement a deal.

Example 3

Weak (not engaging): "It is a market reality that some customers are more profitable than others, to optimize our EBITDA return in this market the decision has been made to rationalize our client book to increase yield."

Strong: "My point is this: we have been bleeding market share too long, and the time has come to deal only with our high-performing customers."

When you create a clear message, you are well-positioned to reach your audience. That clarity must be reflected in the language you use. In the weak messages presented above the language is impersonal (Example 1), negative and unfocused (Example 2), and jargon-ridden (Example 3). All three strong versions express the same thought using the language of leadership.

CLOSE WITH A CALL TO ACTION

The third essential element in the Leader's Script is the call to action. Because leadership is the ability to inspire others to act, you must ensure you indicate how your ideas should be turned into action. The call to action comes at the end of your script – and should be used at the conclusion of any presentation, conversation, meeting, or email where you wish to demonstrate leadership.

In your call to action you can:

- **Ask your audience to take action.** You might ask them to commit to implementing your new company strategy, or simply to review a proposal you've provided to them.
- **Outline how you will take action.** In some instances it is you, your team, or your company that will take the next steps; you can indicate what will follow. For example, you could tell the board of directors that you will begin implementing the plan you described to them.
- **Outline the actions you and they must take.** Sometimes both you and your audience must commit to next steps. For example, if you are making organizational changes, you could ask your employees to submit any questions on their minds and then commit to replying to these in the town hall that you are holding next week.

Regardless of which approach you choose, remember that all effective calls to action are both measurable and time-specific. Measurable means you avoid generalities like "I look for your support" and use specific language that will allow you and your listeners to evaluate if everyone is comfortable proceeding, as in, "I am looking for your support to hire two employees at a total salary of $200,000." Time-specific means defining by when the actions must occur. Such specificity is essential for your audience to know what needs to be done and by when. For example, "I need your confirmation of the two new hires by Monday morning."

Here are some examples of both weak and strong calls to action:

> **Weak (too vague):** "So the project will go better if everyone pitches in over the next few weeks, and on a go-forward basis."
>
> **Strong:** "I need everyone to review the project timelines and meet in their working groups by Friday to identify any obstacles to completing this on time."
>
> **Weak (no timeline):** "I need you to write a personal development plan and review it with me and your coach."
>
> **Strong:** "I need you to write a personal development plan and provide it to me by the end of the month. Then, within two weeks

after that, you and I will meet and you will also review it with your coach."

Notice that the language used in these examples is important; in the first example, the weak version uses the passive voice and has unnecessary qualifiers ("so" and "on a go-forward basis"); the strong version uses the active voice and its language is more precise.

PUTTING IT ALL TOGETHER

By having all three elements of the script clear in your mind before you speak, you will be well-positioned to communicate as a leader. You will have thought about your audience, how you want to move them, and what message you need to convey to help them think differently.

That's not to say you must stick word-for-word with what you prepared – in fact, about the only situation where your script would be delivered as planned would be a formal, scripted speech. But having clarity of thought going in will allow you to adapt your subject, message, supporting arguments, and call to action to the needs of your audience. Perhaps your listeners won't buy in to the degree you'd hoped – in that case, scale back your call to action. Or maybe they mount a passionate challenge to your message that ends up convincing you to adopt a new position – in that case, you may work with them to define the next steps!

SUMMARY

Effective leaders always have a script. Sometimes they actually have a written script – for formal opportunities – but most of the time their script is a mental one. It ensures clarity of thinking and allows them to be precise in the ideas they wish to convey to others.

Getting into the habit of scripting yourself may initially feel difficult, but once you internalize this process you will find your communication becomes significantly more effective.

By having a script with a clear subject, message, and call to action, you will be more confident in your delivery and focused in your thinking. But to be truly effective, these elements, and everything else you say, must be delivered with the language of leadership.

NOTES

1. http://www.theguardian.com/world/2013/aug/09/martin-luther-king-dream-peech-history.

9

USE THE LANGUAGE OF LEADERSHIP

Eva was a brilliant portfolio manager. Her boss showed me how the institutional fund she managed had outperformed its peers for over a decade. Yet Eva had a problem – when she would do shortlist presentations to pension fund board members who were considering investing with her, she failed to inspire – often losing out to competitors with less impressive investment returns.

I had Eva deliver her presentation to me. At first I didn't see many glaring mistakes. Eva was focused and precise in her thinking. She seldom wasted words and got straight to the point, and had a clear message and supporting argument. But as I listened to her go on about value investing and "intrinsic vs. market value," I started to doze off. It wasn't that she was boring *per se*, it was just that she wasn't inspiring.

| 1. Adopt the leader's mindset | 2. Script yourself as a leader | 3. Use the language of leadership |

Figure 9.1　Three Steps to Thinking Like a Leader.

She wasn't speaking as a leader – because she wasn't using words that brought her inner passion and conviction to life.

Too many speakers fall into the trap that Eva did. They present clear, well-structured thinking but fail to engage and move their audiences. Often the reason is that they have not used the language of leadership to bring their ideas forward in a way that grabs people and connects with them on a deeper level than the intellectual one. Hence, our third step in the process of speaking as a leader is to use the language of leadership (see Figure 9.1).

As I conducted my interviews, one of the most frequent and common comments I heard was, "I've never thought about the language I use!" This isn't surprising – our choice of words is almost always unconscious. We have been using words for almost our whole lives to express our ideas. We are continually learning new words (my three-year-old won't learn to "leverage" things for a long time, I hope) and discarding old ones ("radical" is just so 1990!). And while we may edit and polish a document for brevity or clarity, the bulk of our verbal communication just . . . comes out.

One of the beautiful things about verbal communication is that it flows. Speakers who struggle for their words are "tongue-tied" or "at a loss for words." We value listening to people for whom words "flow off the tongue" and who are "great conversationalists."

When it comes to leadership, words matter. Whether you are giving a speech where every word will be transcribed and parsed, or having a conversation with a potential hire, the words you choose will determine whether your audiences are inspired by your thinking.

You should view words as a tool that you can use to achieve a purpose – inspirational leadership. But what kinds of words should you use? Which ones should you avoid?

11 WAYS TO USE THE LANGUAGE OF LEADERSHIP

The next 11 chapters of this book aim to answer those questions. Keeping my writing to 11 chapters was a challenge. After nearly 15 years of coaching and teaching leadership communication ... after 50+ hours of interviews for this book ... after reading countless books by other authors on the subject ... I had a long list of guidelines to choose among. Eventually, I narrowed the field by looking for those principles that shape the language I'd seen the best leaders use, that people kept coming back to in our interviews, and that kept appearing in the books I read. I make no claims about the definitive nature of my list; arguments for the inclusion or exclusion of other principles could easily be made. But I am confident that if your goal is to lead through communications, these 11 chapters will provide you with a meaningful look at what the language of leadership looks and sounds like. Here is a synopsis of the eleven chapters and the principles they cover:

- Chapter 10: The Language of Leadership is ... Visionary

  This chapter will provide you with clarity about the kind of words you can use to articulate a compelling vision. Leaders know that bringing a vision to life is one of the most important things that they must do. A vision is a picture of a future that people want to work together to achieve; without a vision a leader has no followers, and without followers a leader has failed to earn the right to lead. Leaders spend time choosing words that make their vision focused and meaningful to their audience.

- Chapter 11: The Language of Leadership is ... Audience-Centric

  This chapter will show you how to analyze and listen to your audiences and then to choose words that will resonate with them. Leaders focus on shaping the beliefs of their audiences so they can move them to take action. To do this they must first understand who their real audience is, what their existing beliefs and feelings are, and the language that will be meaningful to them.

- Chapter 12: The Language of Leadership is … Jargon-Free

  This chapter discusses when to avoid acronyms, buzzwords, and tech-speak – and when to use them. Leaders recognize that they must choose words that are precise and that provide listeners with clarity. While they seek to use clear and conversational language whenever possible, they also recognize that in some situations technical terms can save time and create a common understanding.

- Chapter 13: The Language of Leadership is … Authentic

  This chapter looks at how you can use words that are your own – and will be recognized as such. Leaders strive to be polished but genuine in all situations. They reject impersonal language and rely instead on familiar words they use in everyday situations.

- Chapter 14: The Language of Leadership is … Passionate

  This chapter examines the role that passion plays in inspirational leadership, and how you can use language to infuse it into your speaking. Too often language is clinical and impersonal. The most effective leaders show they are deeply committed to their ideas. They do this by tone of voice and vocal energy, but they also do this by choosing words that convey to their audiences how they feel about what they are saying.

- Chapter 15: The Language of Leadership is … Confident

  This chapter will show you how to avoid unnecessary self-deprecation and instead use language that demonstrates confidence in your ideas. Speakers undermine their thinking with qualifiers such as "it's just my opinion," or "I could be wrong here." Leaders avoid expressions that create an image of indecision or leave doubt in the minds of listeners.

- Chapter 16: The Language of Leadership is … Positive

  This chapter explains the importance of using positive language. Many speakers make the mistake of using negatives to "tell it like it is" or to deliver the "straight goods." Such words seldom inspire and can make listeners defensive. Leaders do not shy away from harsh realities, but they recognize that the overall substance and tone of their language must be positive.

- Chapter 17: The Language of Leadership is ... Direct

  Leaders get to the point, and in this chapter you will learn to use language that allows you to say exactly what you mean. Leaders know that they need to have the courage to deliver their points to listeners, and they choose language that reflects this directness.

- Chapter 18: The Language of Leadership is ... Concise

  This chapter (very concisely) explains how leaders use the fewest words required. Perhaps you've heard the quotation, "I didn't have time to write a short letter, so I wrote a long one instead." Attributed at times to Mark Twain and in other cases to Benjamin Franklin, the quotation illustrates that it's difficult to be economical with words. Leaders recognize that every needless word distracts the listener from the point they are making.

- Chapter 19: The Language of Leadership is ... Professional

  This chapter will show you how to use language that reflects the professionalism audiences expect of leaders. Many speakers try to bond through using overly casual or colloquial language in an effort to sound "real." Leaders recognize that they need to use language that is personal yet consistently professional, and in this chapter you will learn to walk this important line in your choice of words.

- Chapter 20: The Language of Leadership Uses ... Rhetoric

  In this chapter you will learn how figures of speech can help you to bring your ideas to life and make them memorable. Martin Luther King Jr.'s rhetorical question, "How long? Not long ..." repeated over and over in the speech he made at Selma, Alabama, is one example of the power of rhetoric. Another was John F. Kennedy, who said, "Ask not what your country can do for you, ask what you can do for your country." Even modern-day leaders know that rhetorical devices can be put into practice in every meeting, at each presentation, and during all conversations.

GUIDELINES

Now, before you dive into these chapters, here are six important guidelines to keep in mind:

- First, *look for the ways you are already using language to lead.* Self-awareness is the first step when you are identifying your strengths and looking for ways to improve.

- Second, *don't feel pressure to have your language conform to all of the principles discussed here every time you speak!* Think about which principles are most important in each situation you face. If you are delivering difficult messages, your language should be direct and authentic. If you are laying out strategy for the next five years, your language should be visionary and positive. If you are negotiating a tough deal, your language should be confident and audience-centric. Fit the words to the situation.

- Third, *look for the three new ways you can most effectively start using the language of leadership.* By selecting the three chapters that speak to you and implementing their suggestions when choosing your words, you will give yourself a focused list to refer to when speaking. Maybe you want to be more concise and direct. Or perhaps you want your talks to be more visionary. Making these choices will allow you to implement change once you've finished this book.

- Fourth, *remember that preparation is proportional.* Determine how much time to invest based on the scale and significance of the communication opportunity you are preparing for. If you are getting ready for a crucial TED Talk, by all means rehearse and examine every word. But if you are having a five-minute conversation with your team, ask yourself what tone you want to set and what kind of language will assist you in achieving that objective. Proportionality will help you avoid the "analysis paralysis" trap.

- Fifth, *stay true to yourself.* As you read through the suggestions in each chapter, remember that even though leaders use a common language – one which is positive, direct, and authentic, to give three examples – all leaders have their own unique voice. You must stay true to yourself and use language to help you convey your own ideas in your own voice, but in the best possible way. You are never going to sound like Martin Luther King Jr., or Steve Jobs, or Bill Clinton – and your audiences don't want you to. They want to hear you, at your best. Use the language of leadership to do so.

- Finally, *remember that these chapters are exclusively for you to use when leading.* If you aren't leading, you would use different words. After all, you don't need to use rhetoric when having dinner with your partner and children (though you never know, my three-year-old responds well to metaphor), nor do you need to provide your future in-laws with a vision the first time you meet them. Instead, use the language of leadership *when you actually want to lead.* A leader who is always "on" is exhausting and inauthentic. But there will be moments when you'll want to convey your ideas using words that will reach and energize your listeners. It is in those moments that you will be very glad you can deliberately use the language of leadership.

Summary

To finish the story of Eva, the portfolio manager, she found the words that enabled her to show her passion for managing money. She decided that she needed to bring a flourish to her words so that her ideas would stand out. She did this by tapping into the power of rhetoric and by using repetition, alliteration, and parallel structure to make her ideas engaging and easy to follow.

Like Eva, you should be deliberate in choosing the kinds of words that will help you bring your ideas to life. When you implement these principles, you will make the choice to use the language of leadership.

Now, let's examine the ways you can do so.

10

THE LANGUAGE OF LEADERSHIP IS . . . VISIONARY

If you were to put together a short list of the world's greatest visionaries, you would have to include Elon Musk at or near the top. Musk, a co-founder of PayPal, is best known for founding Tesla Motors (where he is now CEO and product architect) and SpaceX (where he is the CEO and CTO).

Musk's brilliance is found in his ability to think and dream big – but it's also a reflection of his ability to communicate his vision for the future in a way that inspires others to get behind him. He never misses an opportunity to share his vision(s); in practically every speech, blog post, and media interview, he articulates the future he is trying to create.

When talking about Tesla cars, he doesn't just talk about building better electric vehicles, but instead discusses how "the overarching purpose of Tesla Motors (and the reason I am funding the company) is to help expedite the move from a mine-and-burn hydrocarbon economy towards a solar electric economy, which I believe to be the primary, but not exclusive, sustainable solution."[1]

When he talks about SpaceX, he shares his vision for humanity in space, "Ultimately, the thing that is super important in the grand scale of history is, are we on a path to becoming a multi-planet species or not? ... If we're not, that's not a very bright future. We'll just be hanging out on Earth until some eventual calamity claims us."[2]

And when he introduces a new product – for example, a Tesla battery – he discusses the long-term vision that drives his company, "Our goal is to fundamentally change the way the world uses energy at the extreme scale. We're talking at the terawatt scale."[3]

People are drawn to visionaries like Musk who can articulate what is possible. They are inspired to follow them – and, in Musk's case, to invest in their businesses. In 2014 General Motors earned $3,949,000,000 in profits[4] and, as of this writing, has a market cap of $57B. In contrast, Tesla, which *lost $294M* in 2014,[5] has a market capitalization of $31B. How do we account for this? Since investors buy shares on the expectations of participating in future profits, we can infer that Musk's vision has captured the hearts and minds of those who believe more in his future than the one painted by GM.

Whether you are planning to emulate Musk and start a visionary company, or simply want your employees to feel connected to what you are doing, you need to use language that is visionary. In doing so, you will describe a future that will inspire your listeners to help you create it. Here's how to do it.

USE ASPIRATIONAL WORDS

When you articulate your vision, be sure to use words that paint a picture of a future not yet realized. Over 30 years ago, Howard Schultz used descriptive language to describe his vision for coffee houses in the United States. When he traveled to Italy in 1983, he "became captivated with Italian coffee bars and the romance of the coffee experience. He had a vision to bring the Italian coffee house tradition back to the

United States – a place for conversation and a sense of community. A third place between work and home."[6]

Upon returning he founded Starbucks, which today has opened coffee houses around the world. His vision was instrumental in creating the "third place" that so many take for granted today. That vision was also instrumental when Schultz, after eight years away from the company, returned in 2008 to rescue Starbucks from years of decline. It was also present in 2013, 30 years after the founding of the company, when he stressed, "From the beginning, our vision at Starbucks has been to create a 'third place' between home and work where people can come together to enjoy the peace and pleasure of coffee and community."[7]

In my work with leaders, I find that they are reluctant to use this kind of bold language when stating their visions. Here are three recent examples of this kind of conservative wording:

- The CEO of an IT company that served small to medium businesses said that his vision was for "our company to be an industry leader in cloud computing."
- A forest-products head of production stated that her vision for her company was to have "improved to ISO 9001-compliant within five years."
- The head of an accounting firm stated that "we aspire to be a firm that offers exceptional services to private companies."

Each of these leaders knew they needed a bolder vision, but initially the goals they set forth were not inspiring.

I asked these individuals to spend a bit more time imagining their long-term goals. I asked them to focus on using more descriptive language that would help their audiences get excited. Here are their second versions:

- The IT CEO told me, "I see us as a company that helps our clients thrive in the cloud. We will become their in-house Chief Information Officers and they can focus on running their businesses."

- The forest-products executive described "running our mills in a way that sees us become the leaders in our industry. I envision not only earning regulatory recognition, but being looked to by our competitors – and by manufacturers in other industries – as a source of excellence around manufacturing."

- The accounting managing partner told me, "We will be *the* first choice for any private company that requires accounting and financial advisory services. We will be known for industry-leading excellence when we provide the services they require."

In each case the vision remained the same, but the language used to express the vision led to a richer, more easily understood picture for their audiences.

USE PRECISE LANGUAGE

As a child, I remember having a Magic 8 Ball. I would ask it a question about the future, shake it, and then look into a small window where the answer was revealed. I always remember being frustrated when my questions about dating, school marks, or other important events were met with the response, "Reply hazy, try again."

In the world of work, leaders are expected to do the work of the Magic 8 Ball. They are expected to provide their audiences with a vision of the future that is clear and easily understood. That's why it is crucial to use precise language when articulating your vision.

Here's how Marcella Szel, Chair of the Board at Translink, explains it:

> To me [the vision] has to be described in very specific words. They have to be words that mean something. But they can't be too technical...a vision statement...has to be very clear, very specific to our organization; easily understood by everyone.

Yet this kind of clarity is rare; it's all too easy to find examples of imprecise language when reading corporate vision or mission statements. Here are a few:

"Be the global leader in customer value." [Caterpillar]

"The Gillette Company's Vision is to build Total Brand Value by innovating to deliver consumer value and customer leadership faster, better and more completely than our competition." [Gillette]

"Epson is committed to the relentless pursuit of innovation in compact, energy-saving, high-precision technologies, and through the formation of group-wide platforms will become a community of robust businesses, creating, producing, and providing products and services that emotionally engage customers worldwide." [Epson]

Each of these examples suffers from a lack of precise language. In the case of Caterpillar's vision, this lack of precision is due to using language that is so generic that the vision could be applicable to any company. In the case of Gillette and Epson, the lack of precision stems from the use of inflated language and lack-of-substance jargon.

Now consider the following examples of vision statements, which use more precise language:

"To be the number 1 athletic company in the world." [Nike]

"A world in which every child attains the right to survival, protection, development and participation." [Save the Children]

"To land a man on the moon and return him safely to Earth before the end of the decade." [John F. Kennedy, 1961]

These examples are vivid and powerful because of the precision of the language. They are devoid of jargon and use words whose meanings are clear. The result is that the audience can focus on the vision – not on deciphering what it means.

When you get it right, a vision can make a lasting impression. Frederic Lesage is a lawyer and most recently held the position of Chief

Strategy Officer for the Abu Dhabi National Energy Co., also known as TAQA. Earlier in his career he worked as an Associate at McKinsey & Company, recognized as the world's premier strategic consulting firm. When Frederic described what made McKinsey special, he talked about its vision – and what that meant to him:

> McKinsey's vision, which was contained in its mission statement, had two distinct parts: it was . . . and I'm paraphrasing here . . . to help clients deliver outstanding improvements in performance, and it was also to attract, retain, and develop exceptional people. While it sounds more or less generic now, at that time it was new language and it inspired us.
>
> I think that McKinsey was one of the first organizations to have such a clear vision . . . I can tell you that both parts of this vision drove everything we did. Many McKinsey consultants, me included, were hoping to change the world through having deep, positive impact on their clients' organizations. It's something that that we were passionate about. But we were also passionate about continuing to grow as an individual, continuing to learn. In essence, we wanted to have positive, meaningful impact on ourselves as well. So at McKinsey both dimensions of this larger purpose strongly resonated with us.

It's been years since Frederic worked at McKinsey, but the power of the vision remains. He still remembers the two components of the vision and continues to talk about what they meant to him and his colleagues. That's what happens when you articulate a vision with precise language.

USE WORDS THAT SHOW YOUR EMOTIONAL INVESTMENT

Finally, when you convey your vision, you must show your passion for it and commitment to it. The best way to do so is by choosing words that are personal and emotional.

In their 1996 *Harvard Business Review* article, "Building Your Company's Vision," Jim Collins and Jerry Porras make clear why this kind of emotionally vibrant language is essential:

Passion, emotion, and conviction are essential parts of [how you describe your vision]. Some managers are uncomfortable expressing emotion about their dreams, but that's what motivates others. Churchill understood that.... He did not just say, "Beat Hitler." He said, "Hitler knows he will have to break us on this island or lose the war. If we can stand up to him, all Europe may be free, and the life of the world may move forward into broad, sunlit uplands. But if we fail, the whole world, including the United States, including all that we have known and cared for, will sink into the abyss of a new Dark Age, made more sinister and perhaps more protracted by the lights of perverted science. Let us therefore brace ourselves to our duties and so bear ourselves that if the British Empire and its Commonwealth last for a thousand years, men will still say, 'This was their finest hour.'"[8]

When you share your vision — or the vision of your organization — be sure to use words that show how you and your listeners should *feel* about what you are saying.

Let's look at two examples of how to take a generic vision and then deliver it with language that shows the speaker's emotions.

> **Emotionless:** "To become Florida's industry leader in caring for seniors in their retirement by 2020."
>
> **With excitement:** "I believe that together we can take this company to a place where we are the industry leader in Florida by 2020 — and we'll do it by becoming the first choice for seniors who are looking for a place to retire comfortably."
>
> **Emotionless:** "To become a truly global fertilizer products business that serves clients on all continents."
>
> **With urgency, passion:** "We're at a crossroads — either we get swallowed up by our competitors or we grow and prosper in the global market. Let's choose that path and become a global fertilizer company."

Because a vision is designed to make an audience *feel* inspired by a possible future, you need to use language that reflects how *you feel*. Doing so will help them understand your commitment to and belief in the vision.

Summary

Leaders inspire others to act every time they communicate. They do so by articulating what is possible...by sharing their vision for the future. If you want to lead on any scale you too must begin with vision. As Oprah Winfrey said, "Create the highest, grandest vision possible for your life, because you become what you believe."[9]

Your audiences, too, can be inspired to become what you believe – but only if you use language that shows them what is possible. So choose words that are aspirational, precise, and show your emotional investment, and bring your vision to life.

Notes

1. Elon Musk, "The Secret Tesla Motors Master Plan (just between you and me)," August 2, 2006, Blog Post, http://www.teslamotors.com/blog/secret-tesla-motors-master-plan-just-between-you-and-me.
2. Elon Musk, "Getting to Mars," AIAA Propulsion Conference, August 2011, http://web3.aiaa.org/Secondary.aspx?id=4423.
3. Kirsten Korosec, "Top Five Takeaways from Elon Musk's Tesla Energy Reveal," *Fortune,* May 1, 2015, http://fortune.com/2015/05/01/tesla-energy-reveal/.
4. General Motors Income Statement Annual Report (2014), CSI Market, http://csimarket.com/stocks/income.php?code=GM&annual.
5. http://files.shareholder.com/downloads/ABEA-4CW8×0/3965355638×0× 808854/bb31868e-588e-4e95-b72e-729e88e9e932/Q4'14%20Shareholder %20Letter%20Final.pdf.
6. Starbucks, Company Information, http://www.starbucks.com/about-us/company-information.
7. "An Open Letter for Howard Schultz, CEO of Starbucks Coffee Company," September 17, 2013, http://www.starbucks.com/blog/an-open-letter-from-howard-schultz/1268.
8. Jim Collins and Jerry Porras, "Building Your Company's Vision," *Harvard Business Review,* September–October 1996, https://hbr.org/1996/09/building-your-companys-vision.
9. http://www.goodreads.com/quotes/625783-create-the-highest-grandest-vision-possible-for-your-life-because.

11

THE LANGUAGE OF LEADERSHIP IS . . . AUDIENCE-CENTRIC

A few years ago I was having lunch with Bonita, the head of talent development for a large U.S. retail company. Over coffee, she told me about Marcus, a senior vice president of sales, who could wow customers and win major agreements – but couldn't inspire his sales people to buy into his vision and sales strategy.

Bonita was concerned because sales people kept leaving Marcus's team, and those who stayed reported low levels of employee engagement and even lower confidence in the future. They complained about Marcus's poor communication skills – and a lack of direction. This was surprising to Bonita; Marcus seemed like the last person to be branded with "poor communication skills." He was known as "the magician" for his ability to walk into a customer pitch and pull a rabbit – a deal – out of a hat.

Bonita laid out these facts to Marcus, and asked him to explain why his employees didn't seem inspired by him. If Bonita was expecting sheepishness or even accountability, she was quickly disappointed.

"It's simple Bonita," he said, "my audience isn't smart enough to understand my vision and strategy."

Bonita blinked, trying to process whether she'd heard correctly. "Excuse me?"

"It's true. I did my MBA at INSEAD. I'm the top sales person in this industry. I'm operating on a level that really only our fellow executives can grasp. That's why I've been able to win these huge mandates. And that's why the Board and our executive team are onboard with the vision and strategy I created for the sales organization. They *get it*. But these sales people don't, and that's why they're sales people and not sales executives. They just don't have the intellectual horsepower. And I refuse to dumb down the strategy so they can get it."

Bonita confessed to me that it wasn't the first time she'd dealt with an arrogant, egotistical executive. But it was the first time that she had dealt with one who so openly disdained his audience. She wrapped up the conversation quickly – and then went back to report to the CEO, who was less than pleased.

Two months later, there was a new head of sales in the company – one whose ability to wow the sales force was far exceeded by his desire to understand and inspire them.

What Marcus didn't understand – or care to understand – is that *it is the job of leaders* to reach their followers, and not the other way around. Leaders make it their goal to communicate in a way that inspires others to take action. We have seen that the ability to inspire action is developed – and honed through deliberate practice – by consistently making the conscious choice to inspire, and then by choosing the right words to reach your listeners.

Using audience-centric language should also be a deliberate, conscious process. It involves taking the time to understand your audience and then selecting words that will allow your ideas to be understood and embraced when you deliver them.

Here's how to do it.

BEING AUDIENCE-CENTRIC MEANS KNOWING WHO YOUR REAL AUDIENCE IS

Before you can choose to use words that are audience-centric, you must first identify who your real audience is and how you wish to inspire them.

Beauty is in the eye of the beholder – and so are a leader's words. A message that resonates with one group can alienate another.

That's why leaders know they must do the hard work of determining whom they *really* want to reach – before selecting the appropriate words.

Begin by segmenting your audience into three categories:

1. Those you wish to influence and inspire.
2. Those who are already with you.
3. Those who will never be with you.

You should only tailor your remarks – and your language – to the first segment. Doing so effectively will usually keep the second segment in that camp. The third segment should be ignored.

When you assess your audience through this lens, you may find you have been spending your time choosing words in an attempt to influence the wrong people. I remember working with Erik, the head of internal audit for an international shipping company headquartered in Germany. Erik had a contentious relationship with management; he and the audit committee believed the management team – which included the CFO and CEO – were lax when it came to risk assessment. (In my experience, given the internal tension between audit and management, this is not an uncommon perception.) During a coaching session, Erik was preparing for a presentation to the management team. He explained his feelings to me:

"I'm just so frustrated with this management team – they are moving on some risks and leaving others behind. I'm going to use some pretty forceful language because we aren't getting full commitment to addressing our recommendations."

I asked Erik to tell me about the makeup of the management team and their level of responsiveness over the last year.

"Well, it's a mixed bag," he began. "Of the eight people on the team, I'd say four of them – the CFO and her leaders – have been most in our corner. They really are behind us and understand the metrics and risks we've been quantifying for them. They've made huge strides in partnering with us. It's the CEO and his operations team who are the blockers. They just aren't behind us."

I asked Erik about whether the arguments and language he'd been using would have resonated with those individuals.

"Now that you mention it, probably not. These are operators and they have disdain for finance-driven metrics – many came up through the shipping ranks and were captains themselves at one point. They tend to be suspicious of what they call 'spreadsheet captains.' It's possible I haven't been speaking their language."

As our discussion continued, Erik realized two things: he had been treating his whole audience as one group, and he had been using the language of the people in that audience whom *he had already won over.* His real audience was no longer the CFO's team – it was the operations' leaders. He set out to begin "speaking their language" by passing up finance-speak and instead focusing on the language they used around safety within shipping operations. This shift allowed him to be better "heard" and led to a more productive dialogue.

Listen to Your Audience So You Can Choose the Right Words

A crucial requirement for leading is understanding your listeners. Leaders cannot use audience-centric language unless they are first willing and able to listen to those whom they wish to inspire.

Here's Serge Roussel, VP of Finance at Pfizer, on the subject:

To me, being a good leader and being inspirational ... is about listening. When you are sitting in a meeting ... if you stop listening to the discussion and prepare your [thoughts] for when you have to speak, you will not be as effective.... It's important to stop thinking about what you are going to be saying or when you are going to be asked to say it. You must be present in the discussion up until the point that you are going to have to contribute, and it is going to come automatically. Just trust yourself.

As Serge points out, leaders don't just sit in meetings focused on their own remarks. They are fully present in the discussion and listen actively. Why? Because doing so gives them access to valuable information that will enable them to tailor and deliver their remarks persuasively.

So what should you be listening for? Once you know your true audience, you should be listening to them so you can:

- **Identify their existing beliefs.** If leadership is the ability to inspire action by shaping beliefs, you must first understand the beliefs of your audience before you can seek to change or strengthen them. What level of interest, resistance, or engagement do they bring to the ideas that you wish to share? Are your ideas top of mind or will they be completely new? For example, if you go into a board meeting intending to ask for approval of a capital project and you hear the board members talking nervously about poor return on capital numbers, you may choose to use language that speaks directly to the returns you estimate you will be able to deliver.

- **Assess their emotional state.** You will be better able to select the words that will resonate with your audience when you understand how they are feeling. Is your audience angry? Excited? Stressed? Happy? Gauging their mood will allow you to decide how to put your case when the opportunity presents itself – or whether you may be better served by waiting for a future opportunity. You will also be able to tell what kind of leadership people are looking for. For example, if everyone is down about a miss in a product launch, they may be looking for someone to pick them up and inspire them to work toward the new deadline.

- **Determine what "language" they speak and respond to.** Every audience speaks a different "dialect." By listening, you can pick up on the words that resonate with the audience and respond accordingly. Does your audience use personal, casual language, or do they prefer formal language? Is the tone in the room understated or do people passionately champion their ideas? The more listening you do, the better you will understand the kind of words that will resonate with your listeners.

This short list highlights only some of the many things you will learn by listening actively before speaking.

BE READY TO SHIFT FROM ONE LEADERSHIP "DIALECT" TO THE NEXT

Being audience-centric in your language means understanding what group you are speaking with, what "dialect" they use, and then adjusting your language accordingly.

In Chapter 2, I talked about one of the few benefits of using jargon: building a shared sense of identity. Whether it is accountants talking about EBITDA, or bankers talking about M&A, or recruiters talking about human capital, language can immediately denote shared knowledge and identity – as long as everyone genuinely shares an understanding of what the terms mean. Because leaders cannot exist in one group alone, they need to adapt to these different groups. Many, if not most, will have picked up several "dialects" as they progress through their careers. The ability to speak the language of these various groups allows them to work with a wide variety of professionals.

Listen to what John King, an executive with a fascinating career path, told me about adjusting the language you use. John has his MBA, has worked in business process outsourcing, and has spent over a decade as a reserve officer in the Canadian military. Currently, John is CEO of Gemma Communication, a contact center company that provides the customer service functions for some of Canada's largest companies. His success has been dependent on his ability to use audience-centric language. In his current role as CEO, he strives to be audience-centric with two very distinct audiences: his employees at Gemma and with the private equity professionals who own his company. Here's John describing the differences between the two groups and how he adjusts accordingly:

[The language used by private equity] is different in a couple of respects [from that used by employees]. First is that they have some objectives that are not common with running the company. These are more strategic, longer-term objectives, and they think much more about the business valuation . . . than those who operate the business. They think about the business as an asset.

[And their language] is different because they talk about things like multiples of earnings and book value, which are less relevant to operators who talk about profit and loss. [Operations people] are not thinking about multiples of earnings. They're not thinking about things like market value of assets. They're not looking at strategic requirements. They're thinking in terms of profit, expenses . . . .

And when it comes to speaking to these different audiences, it's always a speaker's job to create understanding around the terms they use.

[With operations people] I wouldn't talk about the business in the same terms as I talk to the board [or private equity professionals], not because they wouldn't understand it, but because they probably don't have the background.

John makes the point that it is the responsibility of *leaders* to do the hard work of adjusting their language to their audience. As John's words make clear, being audience-centric does not mean "dumbing down" or "simplifying" what is being said; being audience-centric means choosing words that will resonate with listeners. Each audience has its own "dialect," and being able to identify and use that language is fundamental to speaking in an audience-centric way.

USE LANGUAGE THAT SHOWS YOU HAVE HEARD

Finally, when you do go to speak, use words that show your audience you listened to them and heard what they said. This is often easier said than done. Raymond was a successful investment banker whose ability to help secure financing for his clients had made him invaluable within the firm. Yet, despite his proven skills and an impressive work ethic, his career had stalled. The senior partners praised his technical capabilities but said his communication style was holding him back. "He never seems to listen to us," said one. Another described him as "abrasive, arrogant, and dismissive of the ideas of others." Still another said she "didn't like having him in meetings because he doesn't seem to build consensus."

I was brought in to meet Raymond, whom I found to be pleasant and eager to develop his communication skills. He was aware of his reputation and frustrated that it was holding him back. He was also frustrated because he felt the criticisms did not reflect his personality. He considered himself keen to hear and act on the ideas of others, and wasn't sure why he was perceived to be a poor listener.

As soon as we began roleplaying conversations, I saw what might be the problem. Whenever I would be speaking, Raymond would sit and listen patiently. When I finished he would say, "Yeah, yeah . . ." or "Uh-huh . . ." and then abruptly launch into his own point. Here was a typical exchange:

Me: "It seems to me that doing this acquisition just doesn't make sense given the fact that the target company has been losing money for the last three years."

Raymond: "True, very true. But let me just say this is the company you need to win in this marketplace."

And,

Me: "Raymond, I'm looking at this financing and it seems very unlikely we can get more low-interest debt here. We will have to get subordinate financing if we are going to close this deal."

Raymond: "Yeah yeah . . . so let me be clear: we can finance this whole deal with low-yield debt."

When we talked about this pattern, it was clear that Raymond *was listening* but he wasn't using words that showed he had heard. Instead, he just jumped to his point. The result: he was failing to show that he was, in fact, audience-centric.

We worked on using language that showed he had been listening and allowed him to make a smooth transition from the audience's thinking to his own. Here's what Raymond sounded like when he started showing he was listening:

Me: "Raymond, I'm looking at this financing and it seems there's no way we can get more low-interest debt here. We will have to get subordinate financing if we are going to close this deal."

Raymond: "You are right – getting more low-interest debt will prove challenging. I can appreciate that the only option out there seems to be subordinate debt, which I know is less palatable for you. The good news is that there are other lenders out there we can bring on board. And I believe they will enable us to finance this whole deal with low-yield debt."

By replacing his empty listening statements – "yeah, yeah" – with words that showed he understood and appreciated my comments, Raymond laid the foundation for me to hear his message.

You can show you have heard what's being said by using the following kinds of words before launching into your own remarks:

- **Validating/disarming words.** By beginning with "You're right..." or, "It's true..." or, "I agree..." you will show your audience that you have heard something that will serve as common ground. In high-conflict conversations this kind of language lowers tensions and lays the foundation for persuasion.

- **Empathetic words.** You can show you have heard by using words that demonstrate thoughtfulness or empathy. This does not mean naming feelings (e.g., "I can see that you are angry") but instead identifying and sharing the ideas or feelings of your audience. For example, you might say, "If I were you, having missed out on the last three acquisitions, I'd also want to go after this one aggressively." Or, "If I had an employee sue me I'd be angry too."

- **Supportive words.** You can show respect for the person you've just listened to with your words. For example, you could say, "You're right, this will be a tough company to acquire. And I know, Jeff, that you've gone through an M&A process many times before and your instincts on these deals are always good."

There is also one word leaders avoid when making the transition from the audience's remarks to their own: the word "but." I have heard the word "but" referred to (accurately) as the "verbal eraser." It wipes away everything positive that was said prior to its use. It also sets you and your audience at odds by contrasting your position and theirs. Here's an example of a transition with and without a "but":

With: "It's true that our fund did not outperform the index last year. But we are confident we are a compelling investment."

Without: "It's true that our fund did not outperform the index last year. And you're right, relative performance is important. That's why we look at how we've done relative to the index for the last 15 years, and our track record over that time is outstanding. That's why we are confident we are a compelling investment."

Remember: leaders skip the "but" when showing they have listened, and heard.

SUMMARY

Communicating as a leader involves understanding your audience and how you can inspire them. The more deeply you understand, the more easily you will be able to form messages and choose words that resonate with your listeners. Yet, understanding your audience is only part of being audience-centric; leaders know they must use words that show they have listened to and understood what is shared with them. Doing so earns them the right to be heard when their turn to speak arrives.

12

THE LANGUAGE OF LEADERSHIP IS . . . JARGON-FREE

On January 9, 2007, Steve Jobs took the stage at Macworld Conference & Expo or MCE. Though we didn't know it at the time, he was about to introduce a product that would change the world. Here's what he said:

> Every once in a while a revolutionary product comes along that changes everything. And, Apple has been . . . well, first of all, one is very fortunate if you get to work on just one of these in your career. Apple has been very fortunate it has been able to introduce a few of these in the world. In 1984 we introduced the Macintosh. We didn't just change Apple, we changed the whole computer industry. In 2001 we introduced the first iPod. It didn't just change the way we all listened to music. It changed the entire music industry.
>
> Today, we're introducing three revolutionary products at this MCE. One is a widescreen iPod with touch controls. The second is a revolutionary mobile phone. And the third is a breakthrough internet communications device.

So, three things. A widescreen iPod with touch controls. A revolutionary mobile phone. And a breakthrough internet communications device.

An iPod. A phone. And an internet communicator.

An iPod. A phone .... Are you getting it? These are not three separate devices. This is one device, and we are calling it iPhone. Today ... today Apple is going to reinvent the phone.[1]

The audience roared in excitement. The whole feel of the event – even when rewatching it on YouTube – was less of a tech presentation and more of a religious revival. And much of the reason for that was Jobs, and how he cut the jargon and instead used language that inspired.

This was a calculated choice. After all, Jobs could have gone on and on about the technical marvel that Apple had produced, using jargon based on techno-speak. He could have listed any of the following features about the iPhone:

Form factor:	Slate
Dimensions:	115 mm H, 61 mm W, 11.6 mm D
Weight:	135g
Operating System:	iPhone OS 1.0
CPU:	Samsung 32-bit RISC ARM1176JZ(F)-S v1.0 620 MHz Underclocked to 412 MHz
Memory:	128 MB eDRAM
Storage:	4, 8 or 16 GB flash memory
Battery:	Built-in rechargeable Li-ion battery 3.7 V 1400 mAh

But he didn't.

He eschewed jargon and chose language that was clear, conversational, and vastly more inspiring. Jobs recognized that his goal was not to *inform* people about the product he was introducing but to *inspire* them about what it would deliver. He then chose the jargon-free words that helped him convey that inspirational thinking.

Even if you aren't Steve Jobs, you can learn from his example. Leaders must be focused on inspiring action through communication – and should make their language jargon-free.

Here's how to do that.

COMMIT TO USING THE LANGUAGE OF LEADERSHIP

Begin by making the conscious choice to cut out needless technical terms and acronyms and use the language of leadership. Time and again during my interviews, executives stressed how important it is to make the decision to remove jargon if you want to be heard.

Here's Geri Prior, CFO at the Insurance Corporation of British Columbia, who told me:

> If you want to be heard – and by heard I mean understood – work to get the jargon out of your speaking.

Here's Jay Rosenzweig, President and CEO of Rosenzweig & Company:

> Strip as much lingo and trendy catchphrases and even the so-called intellectual and sophisticated language or complicated words out of your message.... Even if you're presenting to deeply brilliant PhD types, it doesn't matter. Don't try to impress your audience with fancy words or clever language or the latest buzzwords. Keep it clean, keep it simple.

Now, Geri's and Jay's advice may seem self-evident, but in my experience it is not commonly practiced because it requires hard work to self-assess one's language and find jargon-free alternatives. There can be other reasons why we hesitate to go jargon-free. As you recall, in Chapter 4 we looked at inflation-based jargon, which can serve as a cloak of expertise. The story that follows illustrates why this benefit can make it challenging to relinquish jargon.

Virginia, whom I had been coaching for some time, was a senior finance professional in a telecommunications company. She was viewed as a strong technical expert but not yet as executive material. Her boss had told me he always felt he and the other executives had to do "mental translation" when she spoke.

Discussing the company's contact center she referred to "negative trending metrics impacting average call handle time," "leveraging our IVR to drive more ARPU," and "making sure we hit all the KPIs in our SLA." Eyes glazed over.

But Virginia was reluctant to abandon her techno-speak because, as she put it, "[I am] worried that my ideas will sound simplistic and not reflective of the expertise that got me to the table." Virginia was, like many professionals, wearing her jargon as a cloak of expertise.

I challenged her to think about the executive role she aspired to, and how her success in that position would stem from her ability to share thinking that inspires. We made a deal – she would go "jargon-free" in senior-level meetings for two weeks and see what the results were.

Two weeks later she came back excited. "When I started speaking, I was very nervous because my ideas seemed so *basic* without technical terminology. And I became more anxious when the executives actually started asking me questions about my ideas, challenging me to defend them and to explain how I'd arrived at my recommendations. Like when I told them our numbers showed that we could cut $10M in costs if we could just show people how to set their email up when they bought their phones, rather than waiting for them to call into our customer care line for help after the fact."

What Virginia learned was that choosing to go jargon-free is a conscious choice. It takes courage because jargon is often the language of day-to-day business. Using it can mark you as an insider. Yet, the most effective leaders recognize that getting to the essence of an idea is vastly more important than fitting in.

REPLACE JARGON WITH SUBSTANCE

Once you've made the decision to go jargon-free, turn a harsh spotlight on your words to determine which ones can be replaced by more meaningful language. The key is to replace jargon with clear words without sacrificing the meaning you are trying to convey. Here are some examples of this drive for clarity:

Jargon: We need to solution for our human capital maximization strategy.

Clear: We need to find a way to help our employees be more productive.

"To solution" becomes "find a way." "Human capital" is replaced by "our employees." And "maximization strategy" is better said as "helping employees be more productive."

Now for another example:

Jargon: Roadmap mobilization enables the strategy to be socialized with stakeholders, as well as conducting the necessary program planning to begin execution.

Clear: If we communicate our plan, we can find out what people think of the strategy and get everything in place to actually start executing it.

"Roadmap mobilization" is better said as "communicate our plan," while "socialized with stakeholders" is replaced by "find out what people think."

REMOVE UNNECESSARY OR MEANINGLESS JARGON

In the previous two examples, we replaced jargon with clear, substantive language. But doing this kind of term-by-term replacement is not always possible; in some instances, whole sections of jargon must be stripped away to ensure that what remains is substantive. Consider the following two examples:

> **Jargon:** We need to be optimizing things here. We need to be moving to optimize our market-leading footprint if we're going to grow in our vertical. I'm talking about net net being able to increase penetration on a go-forward basis on every single one of our strategic client relationships.
>
> **Clear:** We need to sell more to our biggest clients if we are going to remain a market leader in our industry.

Or this example:

> **Jargon:** Blue-sky with me here people … and think of your balanced scorecards as you go through the exercise to really focus you on long-term value creation in the enterprise. I want you to project the possible, because at the end of the day, it's all about how you leverage your own personal human capital to realize your ability to hit those KPIs.
>
> **Clear:** Think of how you can meet your targets and help the company at the same time.

Leaders strip away all the excess jargon because they want to deliver ideas that are clear and focused to their audiences.

DEFINE WHAT IS LEFT OVER

When you've made the decision to use the language of leadership, replace jargon with English, and delete all that can't be replaced, you may find that there are but a few words left over. If there is no easier way to say it, you can choose to use jargon, but you must first define for your audience exactly what you mean.

Take the term "Q1." Years ago we worked with a company whose goal was to "be Q1." The CEO, COO, and CFO took every opportunity to pound the table and say, "We will be a Q1 company." When we started working with the company's senior management team, we asked different executives to explain Q1 to us. After all, we would be helping them develop and convey clear messages about becoming Q1 to the organization. What exactly did they mean?

The VP of finance was unequivocal: "It means we need to be in the top quartile of performance based on our financial scorecard."

The SVP of operations had a slightly different viewpoint: "Basically, we want to be in the top 25 percent in our industry based on our stock performance."

In search of clarity, we asked the head of marketing for her answer. "Well," she said candidly, "I'm not exactly sure, but we do need to get better in a lot of areas."

Armed with this knowledge, I met with the CEO and told him what I'd learned. He was aghast and embarrassed since he realized he had never defined Q1 for the organization. The next day he called an executive meeting to apologize, and to provide total clarity about what "Q1" meant – which was to be in the top quartile in performance when compared to industry peers. The performance metrics were the ones that each company reported on, including profitability, return on capital, and safety, among others. The CEO provided the organization with a slide that summed up these measures of success, and where the company currently ranked. Once the senior management team understood the term, they were more able to move the organization forward, working toward common goals.

The CEO's decision to use the term "Q1" was not, in and of itself, a mistake; his mistake was not defining it clearly.

If you have a word that can be used to replace a complex concept, or a collective set of ideas, you should feel free to use it. But using the language of leadership means making that choice deliberately, and then defining the word or expression you've chosen to use for your audience.

This also goes for acronyms. Time and again, clients tell me stories of how their first few months in a new role, job, or company were spent trying to learn what particular acronyms meant. Leaders recognize that the onus is on them to communicate clearly. That's why the rule is simple: feel free to use acronyms without defining them if you are positive that everyone in the room will know what they stand for. Otherwise, take the time to define the acronym for your audience.

Be Vocal about Ditching the Jargon and Enlist Others to Do the Same

If your organization is heavy on the jargon, you may have to be more deliberate in signaling that you and the people you work with are going jargon-free. Steve Reid, former Chief Operating Officer at Goldcorp, shared this story with me:

> [I remember] a special project that I led where a small, specialized team was going to work on a specific subject for about six to nine months. We got this team together. We were doing the motivating, aligning, inspiring, and trying to fit some ground rules. We developed small signs and diagrams to place in our office, where this team would meet on a regular basis. One of the things that we had, for example, was to ensure that cell phones didn't distract and detract from the meetings. So we had a little sign with a cell phone with a slash through it. That was one. We had this other one that said TLA with a slash across it (see Figure 12.1).
>
> Everybody would come in and they would look at all our signs, and the way we were operating, and think that is an interesting group because it was this special project. People would ask, "What are TLAs and why are they banned?"

Figure 12.1 Logos.

He paused. I took the bait and asked Steve what TLA stood for.

"Three Letter Acronym." It was a deliberate attempt to avoid the use of jargon and short-cut communication. It was one of those cases where the irony in the message got to reinforce the message.

Steve's story is a great example of how a team made a deliberate commitment to going jargon-free. As a small, tightly knit project team, they could have easily defaulted to using acronyms to create a shared social identity and promote expediency, but they rejected those benefits in favor of clarity of thinking and a desire to connect with those individuals in the company who were not part of the project team.

SUMMARY

Jargon gets in the way of leadership because it creates confusion, doubt, and uncertainty in the minds of audiences. It can also bore and even alienate an audience. That's why using the language of leadership requires that you strip away all but the most necessary terminology, and when you do need those terms, provide clear definitions for your listeners.

Leverage that advice on a go-forward basis and you will maximize your leadership utilization. Or, more succinctly: Speak clearly and make your leadership work for you!

NOTES

1. "Steve Jobs iPhone 2007 Presentation," YouTube, https://www.youtube.com/watch?v=vN4U5FqrOdQ.

13

THE LANGUAGE
OF LEADERSHIP
IS... AUTHENTIC

Indra had just been promoted to Vice President of Exploration at a major global mining company, and she was nervous. She knew she was qualified for the job – over the course of a 15-year career, she had built an impressive reputation for being able to analyze ore bodies in ways that had led her company to expand reserves and extend the life of many of its properties. In the often rough world of mining, Indra had earned respect at the many sites she flew into by being a "no-BS" kind of person. She spoke with passion, conviction, and wasn't above using some not-for-print words to make her points with emphasis. It worked well with the mines' general managers whom she needed to convince, and over the years she'd built strong relationships at the sites and operations level.

Yet Indra was nervous because, for the first time, she would have to present an exploration strategy to the company's board. She'd done a dry run with her COO, who had given her some feedback.

"Indra," he said, "your presentation is sound – your numbers are locked in, your recommendations are great, but you need to deliver it with more polish."

When she pressed him to explain what "polish" meant, he elaborated, "You need to drop the casual language and sound more corporate. You can't be saying, 'I wouldn't touch that deposit if you paid me.' You need to use language that sounds executive-like. And you'd better not use any swear words! I know you do that when you chat to some of these board members over dinners but this is a different forum!"

Indra rehearsed extensively. When her time came, she stood up and started speaking.

"Ladies and gentlemen, it is my pleasure to walk you through our go-forward global exploration strategy. We will discuss how we will leverage our current ore bodies to extend reserves and life of mines . . . ."

As she continued to talk she felt more and more anxious. She looked around the room and saw eyes glazing over. She made eye contact with the chairman, whom she had known for some years. He saw her anxiety and kindly intervened.

"Indra," he said, "let's skip the MBA-speak here. We were excited you were promoted because we believe in your ability to find gold where others don't see it." He smiled, "So cut the corporate bullshit out and tell us where you want to drill."

Everyone laughed, including Indra. With the tension broken, she ditched her notes and said, "Well Jeff, since you asked, let me get right to the part where I tell you which mines we should drill – and which ones I wouldn't touch if you paid me."

THE LANGUAGE OF LEADERSHIP IS AUTHENTIC

Indra was lucky that she had an audience that knew her, believed in her, and was willing to help her when she veered away from using authentic language. Without such support, she likely would have used words that were not her own in an attempt to please her audience; the result would have been diminished delivery and a hit to her leadership presence. Yet, far too often speakers fall into the trap of using language that is not authentic – meaning that they use language to play a part or to meet the perceived expectations of an audience.

Such attempts are rarely successful. Audiences are usually able to sense immediately that the speaker's words ring false. Here's Bruce Derraugh, Chief Operating Officer at FirstOnSite Restoration, on how audiences can smell inauthentic language:

> You may be the warmest person in the world but if you are try-ing to talk differently [and are using jargon], people will say, "He sounds like an idiot." But [despite that], how many times have you seen...politicians...[with the best] words coming out of their mouths...[and even though] the speech was perfect...you could obvi-ously say that message was written by somebody else because those were not their words.

And even in those instances where audiences don't notice, they usu-ally see the difference in a future interaction when those speakers revert to their genuine style.

If you want to speak as a leader, use words that are your own. Doing so will allow others to hear your genuine commitment to your ideas.

Here's how you can use authentic language.

STAY TRUE TO YOURSELF AND THE WORDS YOU USE

The first and simplest way to use authentic language is to know your-self. Specifically, you should listen to the words you use in day-to-day professional situations, and continue using those words no matter who your audience is. In the course of my interviews, over and over again I heard executives tell me how important it is to use words that are authentic.

Here's Anna Tudela, Vice President, Corporate Secretary, Regula-tory Affairs and Diversity at Goldcorp, on authenticity:

If I had to choose, [whether] I want people to see me as a trendy individual who keeps up to date with the hipsters and the jargon that is being used at the moment, right now because of the economy, the industry I am in, or whatever is happening... or [whether] I want to feel comfortable with the message that I'm giving to the group that I know I'm addressing and... want them to understand the message that I want to be there with them sharing my experience... [I would choose the latter].

Here's how Guy Jarvis, Chief Commercial Officer, Enbridge, explained it to me:

In terms of how you communicate, in terms of many other things around your own career, you have to know yourself first. I couldn't communicate in jargon even if I tried because... I would come across as not genuine.

Leaders must evaluate the kind of language they use naturally when they are speaking with passion and conviction – and then commit to being consistent in using that kind of language in all their interactions.

Don't switch your words to please an audience. If you are committed to an idea, speak with words that reflect your genuine commitment. The story of Indra shows that audiences crave the "real" you – someone whom they can listen to and have a genuine connection with. Language reflects that connection.

AUTHENTIC LANGUAGE IS PERSONAL LANGUAGE

Another way to ensure you are using authentic language is to make it personal. Using personal language – "I," "we," "us," "you," and so forth – results in a strong human connection between you and your listeners. Remember that leadership is the act of inspiring others to take action; it occurs when you communicate your thinking in a way that changes the beliefs of your audience. Because you are saying to them, "Here is what I believe, and want you to believe as well," you must use personal language to show that you have a strong degree of commitment to your ideas.

Consider the following examples, which demonstrate how much more effective – and authentic – the speaker is when personal language is used.

> **Impersonal:** "The employee base needs to commit to finding ways to reduce costs and make the business more efficient."
>
> **Personal:** "Each of us needs to commit to finding ways to reduce costs and make our business more efficient."
>
> **Impersonal:** "The performance of this team is not up to standards and it's resulting in weaker relationships with customers. Changes need to happen and are possible with commitment."
>
> **Personal:** "The performance of your team is not up to our standards and it's resulting in weaker relationships with our customers. Changes need to happen and they are possible with the commitment of each member of your team."
>
> **Impersonal:** "The strategy is sound and execution must be the focus in the coming year."
>
> **Personal:** "Our strategy is sound and now we must make execution our focus in the coming year."

The personal examples are far more effective because they show the speaker's commitment to the ideas being conveyed. Rather than talking about "the employee base," use "each of us." Rather than talking about "commitment" generally, refer to the commitment of each member of your team." Rather than "the strategy," discuss "our strategy."

Using personal language shows that you, as the speaker, are not just conveying a corporate message but that you are personally invested in your audience's thinking. The result: a more authentic leadership presence.

AUTHENTIC LANGUAGE BALANCES STRENGTH WITH VULNERABILITY

Another way to ensure your language is authentic is to balance certainty with a willingness to admit what you don't know. Here's how Geri Prior, the Chief Financial Officer at the Insurance Corporation of British Columbia, described that balance to me:

> For me, being authentic is demonstrating in a consistent way that you are honest about things. You answer things honestly. You are honest if you can't answer it. You are honest if you have to say, "You know what, that's really not ready for release right now but we will tell you in three months once we get there...." All of that goes in to building up your own reputation as to who you are....

Leaders know that to be strong they must be willing to be vulnerable. This doesn't mean unnecessarily minimizing themselves (see Chapter 15 for more on mincing modifiers), but rather accepting they won't be perfect all the time and using language that reflects that.

Here's how Frederic Lesage explained it to me in discussing the speaking he did as an executive at the Abu Dhabi National Energy Co., also known as TAQA, and having to speak in English, his second language (his first language is French):

> You have to be yourself. You have to be who you really are. Back to my English-speaking abilities – it's a second language to me as you know.... I tripped on a regular basis in my speeches. I'm fine with that. I've accepted that. And people accept that I would do that. So even in town hall meetings in front of hundreds of people, I have made grammatical mistakes. But I think that if my speeches were polished and had the perfect word everywhere, I might impress first timers who've never heard me before. The people who know me though would say...great speech, but that's not genuine...those aren't your words.

Frederic was willing to accept some imperfections in his language and delivery because he knew doing so was more authentic than delivering a speech that was polished but not his own.

Another way leaders can show vulnerability is by using three simple, yet powerful words: "I don't know." While it's true that there are some things you are expected to know (e.g., a CFO on a quarterly analyst call had better know what the earnings per share were), in many other instances leaders are best served by admitting what they aren't sure about. Many executives worry that admitting they don't know something will hurt them in the eyes of their colleagues – but in reality, trying to say you know everything will hurt you more. Audiences will cease to view you as authentic and tune out even those messages you do have confidence in.

Some years ago I was coaching a Partner at an accounting firm whose staff complained of "broken commitments and promises." I listened in to a few of her town halls and noticed a pattern – when pressed for details on how the firm would turn a strategy into action, she rushed to give detailed responses. For example, when asked how the firm would follow through on its commitment to provide mentoring to young Associates, she started sharing ideas that she later confessed were "half-baked" and "created to try to give a good answer." When pressed as to why she had done this, she replied, "I just felt I had to prove we were serious about getting this done, but now I've backed us into a corner on this one because we aren't sure where to get started or even if we're going to hit the mark with our mentoring program."

Three months later at her next town hall, a member of her team asked, "We haven't seen anything on your commitment to mentoring since our last town hall. When are you going to get this rolling?" She paused and replied, "You're right, we haven't done anything yet, and I apologize for that. The reality is we know that we need to take some steps, but we don't know what to do yet. I say that because we haven't spoken to you and your colleagues . . . so rather than me and the Partners cooking something up, we'd like to hear from you about what should go into this program before we get rolling. So, if you don't mind, I'll start by asking you right now . . . ."

The result: the junior staff began shaping the program they were looking for – and the partner was viewed as communicating more authentically.

Summary

While using the language of leadership may seem incompatible with authenticity, the two are one and the same. The most effective leaders speak with the language they use everyday, and admit when they don't have the answer to a particular question. Do that, and your audience will hear you at your best.

14

THE LANGUAGE OF LEADERSHIP IS...PASSIONATE

On September 20, 2014, Emma Watson, the British actress best known for her role in the Harry Potter movies, delivered a powerful speech at the United Nations' headquarters in New York. Her presentation launched the HeForShe campaign, a global movement designed to promote gender equality.

Watson presented a compelling case for gender equality around the world. And people listened: at the time of this writing, just eight months after her speech, over 300,000 men (including me) have been inspired to take the "I am HeForShe" pledge to "commit to taking action against gender discrimination and violence in order to build a more just and equal world."[1]

Watson's speech was impressive for many reasons, but the one that stands out is how effectively she conveyed her passion for the cause of gender equality. She didn't do it with a booming voice, fiery gestures, or a commanding physical presence; she conveyed her passion through the words she chose.

Here are some excerpts:

I was appointed as Goodwill Ambassador for UN Women six months ago. And, the more I spoke about feminism, the more I realized that fighting for women's rights has too often become synonymous with man-hating. If there is one thing I know for certain, it is that this has to stop....

I decided that I was a feminist, and this seemed uncomplicated to me. But my recent research has shown me that feminism has become an unpopular word.... Why has the word become such an uncomfortable one? I am from Britain, and I think it is right I am paid the same as my male counterparts. I think it is right that I should be able to make decisions about my own body. I think it is right that women be involved on my behalf in the policies and decisions that will affect my life. I think it is right that socially, I am afforded the same respect as men.

But sadly, I can say that there is no one country in the world where all women can expect to see these rights. No country in the world can yet say that they achieved gender equality. These rights, I consider to be human rights, but I am one of the lucky ones.

And, later on, she continues:

Both men and women should feel free to be sensitive. Both men and women should feel free to be strong. It is time that we all perceive gender on a spectrum, instead of two sets of opposing ideals. If we stop defining each other by what we are not, and start defining ourselves by who we are, we can all be freer, and this is what HeForShe is about. It's about freedom.

In closing:

You might be thinking, "Who is this Harry Potter girl, and what is she doing speaking at the UN?" And, it's a really good question. I've been asking myself the same thing.

All I know is that I care about this problem, and I want to make it better. And, having seen what I've seen, and given the chance, I feel it is my responsibility to say something.

In my nervousness for this speech and in my moments of doubt, I told myself firmly, "If not me, who? If not now, when?" If you have similar doubts when opportunities are presented to you, I hope those words will be helpful.[2]

In reading Watson's remarks, you can hear her commitment to ending inequity, her indignation that women are not given the same rights as men, and even her nerves around having to take up the mantle of ambassador. In short, her language conveys her passion for her cause.

Watson's use of language to convey emotion is a powerful example of how leaders must not only convey ideas, but what they and their audiences should *feel about those ideas.* Remember: your goal as a leader should be to inspire action. You must define and share your convictions with others, and you should take care to use words that convey the passion you feel for those ideas.

Here's how to choose words that will allow you to express your passion effectively.

EMBRACE PASSION

The first step is to get comfortable with the idea that you can and should show passion when speaking. In my years of coaching executives, I have found that many individuals are often reluctant to express their passion overtly. There are a number of reasons for this hesitation. One common reason is that passion can often be associated with "selling" an audience something they don't need.

Haylee was a senior manager in a global consulting firm, and her specialty was implementing strategic sourcing for international oil and gas companies. She had great expertise in working with suppliers and finding opportunities for cutting costs. She could present that information with clarity and confidence.

But Haylee had also been passed over for promotion to director. When she sought feedback she was told that the Partners liked her but didn't feel she could independently represent the firm when they pitched for business. She was too "flat" in her delivery and until that changed they would hold her back. Haylee asked if they would support coaching to address this shortcoming, and when she got the go-ahead I began working with her.

In our first roleplaying session, I saw what the Partners meant. She stuck to the facts, and presented them clearly but with little energy or enthusiasm. When I asked her to try "turning up the dial" she resisted, telling me, "I'm comfortable with the facts. They are what I can stand on – they represent the foundation of my talk. I'm not here to sell anyone or be a huckster, and I won't compromise my integrity for the sake of a deal."

We dug deeper into this perspective. I learned that Haylee felt that at several points in her career she herself had been "sold" by passionate people who ultimately didn't deliver. She'd taken an internship out of university that ended up being more of an unpaid job; she'd moved in with a friend whose passion for co-habitation waned when the reality of sharing chores set in; she'd taken a "stretch assignment" working for a charismatic leader who promptly ignored her when she moved to England to work on his project team. Through these and other experiences, Haylee had become deeply wary of people who tried to "sell" others, and she had resolved neither to be fooled again nor to fool anyone herself.

I asked Haylee about the presentation we were roleplaying, and what her recommendations were. She was reluctant at first, saying her job was to present the data and for the client to make the decision. I tried another tack and asked her what she would do if it was her company. She replied, "Well, I would drive out 70 percent of the vendors here and implement centralized procurement policies. Then I would demand a reduction of 15 percent from those vendors we kept. It's shameful the way the vendors are 'dividing and conquering' this company and I'd do something about it."

Suddenly aware of her emotion, she apologized! But I asked her if what she had said was genuine and based on the facts. She confirmed it was. We then discussed how the people who had "sold" her in the past had not had the facts on their side – they had used passion to convince her of something that was not backed up by reality.

By the end of our session Haylee agreed that, if she did feel the information warranted it, she would be willing to try speaking with more passion to show how she felt about the data. It was the beginning of a new mindset for her. If you are like Haylee and are uncomfortable "selling" through language, then focus on only sharing your passion when you believe fully in the message you are delivering. This will allow you to speak with integrity.

Another reason you may be reluctant to show your passion is that getting emotional at work is often viewed as a loss of control. It's important to recognize that some emotions – such as anger – do have negative ramifications for leaders and should be avoided. But more broadly, emotions are essential for successful leadership.

Here's Anne Kreamer, author of *It's Always Personal: Navigating Emotion in the New Workplace*, explaining this in a *Forbes* article:

> Since the recent study of emotion, we're beginning to understand that the old-school sense of the workplace as rational and everything outside it as appropriate for emotions couldn't be more wrong.... In the workplace, whether you're pitching a new concept or negotiating a deal, emotion is involved and important.[3]

The sooner you recognize that passion can help you as a leader, the more effective you will be.

Les Dakens, former human resources executive at Heinz, CN Rail, and Maple Leaf Foods, explains it this way:

> If I want to inspire you, I have to be emotional with my language so that you and I could connect at that level and say, "Right, let's high five and let's do it." In most cases, I want to do that if I'm trying to inspire you, motivate you.
>
>   Now, if I am trying to correct your behavior, I may use emotion but it might be perceived as more anger. I want to be very careful of that. Because at some point, the anger can get translated as far more personal in terms of the receiver and your action may intimidate that person – they just want to leave.

So passion is most effective when you're trying to positively inspire someone.

Finally, people may be reluctant to show passion because it may feel like a disingenuous "performance." I often hear this from leaders who are low-key and who prefer to build support for their ideas in an understated way, over time. While such an approach may work, it's not always the best way to convey to your audience that you are committed to an idea. Since leadership *is* a performance, it is good to remember that you are always on stage, and that playing the part effectively means being able to show your passion. The key is to perform authentically.

USE PASSION TO SUPPORT YOUR LEADERSHIP GOAL AND MESSAGE

Once you're comfortable with the idea of conveying your passion, you should focus on doing so in service of your leadership message. Use your passion to highlight how you feel about the ideas you are conveying, and how your audience should feel.

Here's Chuck Fallon, CEO at FirstService, talking about his own passionate style and how it works when he channels it in support of a strategy he believes in:

> I'm a sucker for motivational inspiration.... And so I guess, I've been a little lucky, but I get excited. I'm Irish; I have got a bit of a temper. Somehow that manages to find its way to the emotion that I bring on. And so that, to me, is fun. And it's one of the hardest things to do. Defining what those four pillars are [of our strategy] and make sure they resonate every day. But if that's what makes your socks go up and down then that's [great].

Here's David Gibbons, Managing Partner at Korn Ferry, talking about the importance of passion when communicating:

> I am very purposeful in conveying passion because I find that people's engagement with what you're talking about has a lot to do with

the energy that you're bringing, and so, for me, just recognizing the importance of passion makes the difference in how I approach my communication.

In client meetings I'm very aware that the energy needs to be there. I find that it's a virtuous cycle in that the more I get excited about [the topic], the more other people get excited about it, and then the more I get excited about it.

David's choice of the word "purposeful" is significant; you should not allow passion to spill out uncontrolled. Instead, consciously use it in service of your message.

Toms Lokmanis is Vice President, Business Development at Caledon Capital Management, a private equity and infrastructure firm. Toms explained that when it comes to showing passion,

You can't play things to chance, you really have to practice. There are certain things you really need to [have clarity about] – and you need to practice them…so you get the clarity of thinking you need to show your passion.

Toms makes a great point – though we often think of emotion as spontaneous, you have to know *ahead of time* what you plan to say so you know you can speak with passion *in the moment*. How do you get this kind of clarity? You have it when three key things are clear in your mind:

- The action you want to inspire your audience to take;
- The belief you want to leave them with;
- The feelings you and they need to have that will lead them to take action.

Let's look at an example. Let's say you are a project manager in an engineering construction company. You want to inspire your project team to work intensely over the weekend to meet a deadline. That effort will allow your company to meet the commitments it has made to the client.

You *could* say, "Team, we need to come in this weekend and wrap up this section of the construction or we will miss our deadline. I'll see you Saturday."

While accurate, this message is not inspiring. Let's look at how you can connect to your passion to increase the effectiveness.

You give some thought to why you *feel* it's important to come in on the weekend and deliver. You know that you don't feel it's a burden but instead something you want to do. You think about how the value of integrity governs how you work and how you live, and how you *feel passionate* about meeting the commitment you made to that client, even if it means working on the weekend.

And then you say, "Team, we need to come in this weekend to wrap up this section of the construction because we made a commitment to this client. I wouldn't ask you to come in if it wasn't something I felt very strongly about doing. That's because I believe that in business and in life, when you make a promise, you deliver. And we promised this client we'd hit this deadline. I'll see you Saturday."

By connecting to the emotion that drove your decision and by communicating that emotion, you end up with a more engaging message.

❧

EXPRESS YOUR PASSION OPENLY

Once you've decided to express your passion, do so openly and publicly. The easiest way to share your passion is to tell everyone how you feel. Here are some examples:

No emotion: "I'll be presenting our strategy to you today."

Emotion: "I'm excited to present our strategy to you today because our whole management team is committed to it and invested in its success."

No emotion: "You did not meet your targets and you should have."

Emotion: "I'm disappointed that you did not meet your targets, because I believe you have all the capabilities to have done so."

No emotion: "We are here to go over the quarterly financial numbers."

Emotion: "We are here to go over the quarterly financial numbers, and I am proud of what we have achieved together."

Don't stop at just naming your feeling – explain it for the audience. Doing so allows them to connect with the ideas you are conveying on a deeper level. Here's an example from Lebron James, perhaps the greatest basketball player in the world:

> I hate letting my teammates down. I know I'm not going to make every shot. Sometimes I try to make the right play, and if it results in a loss, I feel awful. I don't feel awful because I have to answer questions about it. I feel awful in that locker room because I could have done something more to help my teammates win.[4]

James's overtly emotional language allows us to hear his passion and shows how it is channeled not toward his own success but toward the success of the team.

Summary

If you want to lead, you must be able to identify your passion – and convey that passion to your audiences. Get comfortable with the benefits of using passion and make the choice to do so when you speak. Then identify your audience, your message, and your emotion about that message. Finally, convey your passion boldly and publicly.

Notes

1. "The HeForShe Commitment," A Solidarity Movement for Gender Equality, http://www.heforshe.org/.
2. Emma Watson, "Gender Equality Is Your Issue Too," September 21, 2014, UN Women, http://www.unwomen.org/en/news/stories/2014/9/emma-watson-gender-equality-is-your-issue-too.

3. Jenna Goudreau, "From Crying to Temper Tantrums: How to Manage Emotions at Work," *Forbes,* January 9, 2013, http://www.forbes.com/sites/jennagoudreau/2013/01/09/from-crying-to-temper-tantrums-how-to-manage-emotions-at-work/; Anne Kreamer, *It's Always Personal: Navigating Emotion in the New Workplace* (New York: Random House, 2013).

4. "10 Lebron James Quotes on Being the Greatest," http://www.fearlessmotivation.com/2015/05/21/lebron-james-quotes/.

15

THE LANGUAGE OF LEADERSHIP IS . . . CONFIDENT

Confident language is a necessity when you're closing a deal. Here's a cautionary tale illustrating that point. Steve, a senior manager in a major accounting firm, was focused on privately held companies. He felt his accounting firm should expand their work with those companies, and he pitched the idea to his bosses.

"I'm sorry to be taking you away from your clients because I know this is a busy time and you are all swamped."

He paused. The Partners looked at each other. One said, "You're right, so I hope this won't take long!"

"Oh, don't worry, it won't," said Steve, laughing awkwardly. "It's just that there may be something you'd want to know about the private company market. I could be wrong on this one, but I think we might have just a bit more upside there if we'd focus our efforts on these companies rather than competing for the tightly contested public market business. But in the end I know you all probably know way more about this than I do . . . ."

There was a pause. One of the Partners replied, "Well, Steve, I'm sure you've done some good work but we do feel we know more on this one, so let's just stick with our strategy for now."

The meeting wrapped up and Steve went away crestfallen that his audience hadn't wanted to hear more.

Steve's story is an example of the pitfalls of using language that suggests you lack confidence in your ideas. His audience was not fully to blame for not drawing him out. They listened to the words he chose and evaluated Steve's level of conviction in his position. What did they hear? That Steve himself seemed unsure about the opportunity in private companies. The result: they decided that *if Steve wasn't sure about the opportunity, they shouldn't waste their time listening.*

Now, if Steve *wasn't sure* that would make sense, but the problem in this instance was that he *was sure* that there was a compelling opportunity. Yet he used language that sent the opposite message.

THE LANGUAGE OF LEADERSHIP IS CONFIDENT

Leaders are focused on inspiring action. They want others to hear their ideas and adopt them as their own. To do this they need to present their ideas as ones that are worthwhile adopting. The language of leadership is therefore confident.

Here is what Toms Lokmanis tells me:

> It's crucial that leaders project confidence because leaders must inspire change and motivate their audience. In the age of information overload and limited attention spans, it is critical to engage your audience by delivering a well-scripted and engaging message.

Using confident language does not mean using language that is arrogant, boastful, or unnecessarily strident. Such choices will undermine the speaker. Using confident language means choosing words that help your audience feel the level of conviction you have in the ideas and information you are sharing with them. It means avoiding unnecessary qualifiers or "mincing modifiers" that diminish the strength of your ideas.

In Steve's remarks he added on expressions like "I could be wrong on this one" and "I think we might have just" to his more substantive ideas. The result was the audience wondered why they should have confidence in his ideas when he didn't seem to have it himself.

Here's how you can use confident language.

GET CLEAR BEFORE YOU GET CONFIDENT

It may sound self-evident, but if you want to use confident language, you first need to feel confident! Confidence comes from clarity of thinking. As I discussed in the introduction to Part II, leaders do a lot of mental work before they speak. This work is focused on defining who their audience is, what action they wish to inspire, and what message they want to convey.

Recently, I helped Phillippe, an investment banker, prepare for a presentation to the board of directors of a company that he was advising. He had to provide his analysis on an unsolicited offer they had received. I recorded his first cut at the talk:

> Well, I've had my analysts crunch the numbers and there's a lot to consider. Definitely at the lower end of the valuation range relative to similar market transaction. So I'm not sure we should get too excited. Then there's the asymmetric nature of the relationship here, since the buyer operates the asset and really knows what it's worth. But at the same time, they are a strategic buyer which makes them the most likely acquiring party. So it looks like this could be our best shot, and maybe our only shot.

When I played back the pitch to Phillippe, I asked him to assess the level of confidence the board would have based on that pitch.

"Well, frankly," he responded, "I don't see them feeling confident at all. I came off totally unclear and, consequently, I sounded like I was arguing both for and against the deal."

I agreed and asked him to take a few minutes to get clear on his position and his recommendation, and then to try it again. Here's what came out:

> My team and I have looked at this offer, and our conclusion is that while this is an imperfect offer, it's one we should strongly consider. Here's why. The buyer is the operator, which means they will likely pay more. They are also our only likely buyer because no independent acquirer would be interested. Also we should be able to raise the valuation. For those reasons, our recommendation is to proceed with the dialogue.

As Phillippe realized, when it comes to language, clarity drives confidence.

◈◈◈

COMMIT TO YOUR POSITION (DON'T HEDGE)

When leaders speak, audiences follow. Yet, no audience wants to follow those who are unsure of their position. Here's Michael Morrow, a Partner and Senior Managing Director at Deloitte, explaining it to me:

> The type of language that shows lack of confidence is imprecise language, where you stumble around topics. So you're trying to talk to a certain topic and you can't articulate it clearly and therefore you're fumbling your way through it, I find it demonstrates you don't know what you're talking about.

Michael went on to explain that even those who did have confidence in their subject matter could undermine themselves through their language, creating the perception they were unsure of themselves:

> The funny thing is that sometimes people are just not naturally as articulate as others. They may be fumbling their way through something but it's not because they don't know what they're talking about.

Perception is reality – you need to commit to your position when you speak for your audience to feel confident in your ideas. This is why leaders know they must use language that reflects a commitment to their ideas. Consider the following statements:

- "We can't know for sure who will win the game, but based on the Dallas Cowboys' terrible record this year, I'm confident the Philadelphia Eagles will prevail. That is, of course, assuming that the Cowboys don't catch fire because they have nothing at stake and play loose. In fact, that is a likely scenario because they thrive when the pressure is off. So it could go either way."

- "Based on the focus group research we should launch this new hair product now, because it is likely that it will appeal to the teen market. But as we all know, focus groups are notoriously poor predictors of market adoption of a product. It's just hard to know whether we should push our chips in now or wait a while longer."

Does either example make you feel inspired – to back one team over the other or to make a decision about launching a product? Are you drawn to either speaker's commitment? Not really.

If you want to inspire others to take action based on your ideas, you must first show your commitment to those ideas through the use of confident language. Take all the time you need to arrive at a conclusion in your own mind – and then eliminate any language that would cast doubt in your audience about your own commitment to that conclusion.

CHOOSE WORDS THAT REFLECT YOUR ACTUAL LEVEL OF CONFIDENCE

Leaders use language that is confident – but, more importantly, that reflects the *level of confidence* they have in what they are saying. Here's an example of how too much confidence can alienate a listener:

Overconfident: "There is only one way to reengineer this process and I know that for a fact because I've done it this way successfully."

Appropriately confident: "Based on my expertise, I'm confident this is an effective way to reengineer this process."

The overconfident language ends up sounding arrogant. A listener would consider it unreasonable if someone were to say that there is "only one way" or "I know that for a fact."

In the following example, we see again how using unrealistically confident language undermines the speaker:

Overconfident: "If you invest the capital in our business, we will dominate this market and make everyone a ton of money – I guarantee it."

Appropriately confident: "We believe with your capital and our expertise we are well-positioned to make meaningful inroads in this market."

Bombastic language like "dominate this market" and "I guarantee it" does not reflect leadership because it either misrepresents the speaker's confidence or (perhaps worse) reflects an inappropriate level of confidence.

But get it right. As the discussions that open this chapter make clear, a lack of confidence is an equally grave failing. Consider these examples:

Not confident enough: "I'm not sure this candidate is the right one for us . . . one can never be sure if someone will work out . . . but let's make her an offer."

Appropriately confident: "While every candidate – including this one – has flaws, I've seen enough to say I believe we should offer her the position."

BE CONFIDENT, NOT ARROGANT

Confidence is desirable in leaders, but overconfidence and arrogance are not. Even if you are supremely confident in an idea, be cautious about using language that may position you as arrogant or disinterested in the views of others.

Gregory was an Associate at a respected management consulting firm. The firm's principles convened a call to discuss strategies for growing client relationships. One Partner suggested that you needed champions at both the executive level and in the supply chain office to secure engagements. Another Associate agreed, though she wished that there was a single decision maker whom she could land deals through. Then Gregory spoke, "Well, I've had a lot of success and I can tell you there is always one person who you need to find and win over, and if you do that you will get your deal."

There was silence on the line. The Partner leading the call said, "Gregory, in some instances there is one person, but generally in our experience you need relationships at multiple levels to secure the kind of long-term engagement we are after."

Undaunted, Gregory replied, "No, there is always one person. You just need to find them."

The call wound down…and within a few months, so too did Gregory's career with the firm.

In this instance Gregory was very clear and confident in his position. He chose language that accurately reflected that confidence. Yet his confidence positioned him as someone who was not willing to value the experiences and expertise of others.

Be sure to choose language that reflects confidence while still demonstrating your respect for, and openness to, other points of view.

Eliminate the Mincing Modifiers

One of the easiest ways to use the confident language of leadership is to eliminate the "minimizing" modifiers that so many of us use without realizing it.

Anna Tudela, Vice President at Goldcorp, identified this type of language as a barrier to projecting confidence. She explained that many people use expressions such as,

"I think," "in my opinion," "I'm sorry," "my apologies"….

The people who use these phrases constantly [come across] as unsure of their ideas and don't express their ideas with certainty. The result is they and their ideas get ignored. If you have an idea and you believe in your idea – you have to be firm about it! And you have to say, with confidence, "I truly believe that this is the way to go and these are the reasons why!"

If you use words like "I think," "perhaps we could," or something along these lines... [if] I use those type of words I will lose the confidence of my [audience] and they will see me as someone insecure who can't make a decision. Forget it. You might as well not make any suggestions at all.

Anna is correct: mincing modifiers undermine your ability to project confidence. That's why you need to be conscious of how these words minimize the meaning of your message and deliberately purge them from your speech.

A short list of mincing modifiers includes:

Just

Sort of

A bit

Perhaps

Probably

I think

I'd guess

We might

It could

There are, it's true, times when you want to convey your uncertainty and you might want to use one of the terms. But always do so with great care.

Far more often in our work with clients we find that speakers are unconsciously using these words, and in doing so are unintentionally weakening their leadership. In a session with Julia, a railway safety supervisor, I asked her to describe the solution she was preparing to present to management. Here is what she said:

> Well, I just wanted to take a few minutes of your time to talk about what we can do to bring down the injury rate by our track maintenance crews, if that's OK with you? I can't be sure, but it's maybe just a case of getting away from a culture of kind of maybe penalizing them for misses and instead encouraging them to bring misses forward. We might want to look at culture rather than process, I guess.

After she was finished speaking, I asked Julia to tell me on a scale of 1 to 10 – with 10 being highly confident – how confident she felt about culture being the driving reason behind the incidents. When she told me "7 or 8," I played back the tape and asked her to rate how confident she sounded. Her reply: "2 or 3." Then I played it again and asked her to count the mincing modifiers. The total: 9 (see if you can find them all). Then she tried it again:

> I'd like to talk to you about bringing down the injury rate on our track maintenance crews. I'm confident that a likely solution will involve changing the culture in these crews so people don't feel punished for safety misses. We want them to feel supported and encouraged to identify safety gaps. I believe a culturally based approach, rather than a procedural one, will give us the best chance at success.

Same content. No mincing modifiers. Much higher projected confidence.

SUMMARY

Leaders who wish to inspire their audiences must first get clear on their positions, and then use language that reflects their confidence. By doing so, they signal to their readers and listeners their key message: "I believe in this idea and you should too."

16

THE LANGUAGE OF LEADERSHIP IS . . . POSITIVE

Recently, I was conducting a workshop for a group of senior finance leaders in a major financial services institution in downtown Toronto. We were discussing the need to make messages positive rather than negative. The CFO said, "I can't agree more. I remember in 2006, the investment bank had had its most profitable year ever. At the end of the year we brought all our staff together. Our CEO stood up and started talking about the year. And I will never forget what he said. 'We had record results. And I have only three words to describe them. Not. Good. Enough.' In that moment he lost the whole company. For the next three years not one of us wanted to work for him. And we never forgot what he said."

Nearly a decade later, that story was still fresh in the CFO's mind. That one use of negative language had stuck with him, and it had destroyed his confidence in the CEO.

This is an example of why leaders make the choice to lead using positive (yet realistic) language. They recognize that if they want to inspire others to act, they must paint a picture of the future that provides hope, and they must provide positive perspectives on difficult realities.

People want to follow positive leaders. I asked Jeff Medzegian, Director of Supplier Performance at Boeing, to describe the characteristics of the leaders he'd most enjoyed working for during his 20 plus years at Boeing. He told me:

> I think the better ones are...positive and inclusive...
>
> They're able to articulate what the issues are and why they're so important for us to address. They just pump you up, inspire you to want to go tackle the problems. Whereas some of the ones that weren't so inspiring were more negative on things and pointing out the problems and just trying to motivate through telling you how bad of a job we're all doing and that we got to do better.

But what about telling the "truth"? Shouldn't leaders avoid "sugarcoating" harsh realities or being "cheerleaders"?

The short answer is that leaders need to be positive, yet realistic. Before I look at how to walk this line, let me explain why it's so important that leaders avoid negatives.

THE IMPACT OF NEGATIVES IS GREATER THAN POSITIVES

Research conclusively demonstrates that leaders should avoid unnecessary negatives and instead use language that is positive. The reason is that negatives have a far more detrimental and longer-lasting effect on audiences.

I interviewed Dr Jorina Elbers, who is an Assistant Professor of Neurological Sciences in the division of Child Neurology at Lucile Packard Children's Hospital, which is part of Stanford University in California.

Jorina spoke at length to me about the harmful effects of negative language:

> The impact of negative language – blaming [and] shame producing – is quite damaging especially when it happens on a regular basis. What it

does is that it puts them into a mode where they need to defend them-selves. They actually go into a sympathetic overdrive response, which is they get anxious, their heart rate increases, they go into a fight or flight mode.

When you go into the primitive fight or flight response, you actually shunt blood away from the frontal part of the brain and into the brain stem.

The front part of the brain, or the neocortex, is the new part of the brain that differentiates us from monkeys.... It is essentially the exec-utive function: the planning, the problem-solving, the creative part of the brain. When you take the resources, the blood and the oxygen, away from that and into the brain stem – the brain goes offline.

[The person then] goes into a state where they are protective, they are defensive. Their body goes into a mode where the muscles tense, their heart rate increases, their breathing increases, they're anxious and essentially their thinking brain goes offline.

I then asked Jorina about the implications for leaders who wanted to understand how to be direct without being critical or using damaging negative language. She explained:

By providing criticism or feedback in a way that keeps people online, they will keep people out of the...fight or flight mode. [In this way] the solution or the outcome can be brought out in a creative, thought-provoking manner.

It's not just in the moment where they are delivered that negative comments have a detrimental effect on audiences; long after they have been spoken, negatives will stick in the minds of those who hear them.

In a 2001 *Review of General Psychology* article entitled "Bad Is Stronger than Good," Roy Baumeister and his colleagues reported the following:

Bad emotions, bad parents, and bad feedback have more impact than good ones, and bad information is processed more thoroughly than good. The self is more motivated to avoid bad self-definitions than to pursue good ones. Bad impressions and bad stereotypes are quicker to

form and more resistant to disconfirmation than good ones.... Hardly
any exceptions (indicating greater power of good) can be found. Taken
together, these findings suggest that bad is stronger than good, as a general principle across a broad range of psychological phenomena.[1]

In his book, *Thinking Fast and Slow*, the Nobel Prize-winning
economist Daniel Kahneman explains the reason why humans have
this negativity bias:

The brains of humans and other animals contain a mechanism that is
designed to give priority to bad news. By shaving a few hundredths of a
second from the time needed to detect a predator, this circuit improves
the animal's odds of living long enough to reproduce.[2]

The implications of the negativity bias for leaders and their language
are significant:

- Negatives will be remembered far longer than positives.
- Audiences will perceive speakers who use negatives less favorably
  than those who use positives.
- Audiences will go out of their way to avoid or distance themselves
  from those individuals they perceive as negative.

For these reasons and more, leaders must be conscious about using
language that is positive.

ACKNOWLEDGE NEGATIVES THE RIGHT WAY

When leaders use positive language, they do so without obscuring
harder realities. It is crucial that leaders acknowledge any negative components in their content in the right way. For example, a leader speaking about a new strategy needs to acknowledge that the last strategy
failed to bring about the desired results. A CEO who is discussing sales
targets with the new head of sales should also acknowledge what led to
missed targets in prior years.

Acknowledging negatives allows leaders to deliver a wake-up call that forces an audience to confront the need for change.

- Mentioning negatives enables leaders to show they are not solely focused on whitewashing or "blowing smoke" at their audiences.
- Acknowledging negatives allows leaders to show they are aware of what is worrying the audience, which builds a stronger connection.

These and other outcomes can all support the leader's goal of connecting with an audience to inspire them to act. Yet, negatives must be acknowledged carefully. Specifically, they must be stated in a way that will support the speaker's ability to lead and inspire.

Here are three ways to achieve this:

- **State negatives non-judgmentally.** When speakers use negatives as a weapon to single out or punish certain members of their audience then they polarize their listeners.
- **State negatives without being consumed by them.** Audiences will take their cues from how leaders position negatives; if the leader sounds demoralized or undone, the audience will feel that way too. Conversely, if the leader is acknowledging a difficult reality but sees it as a surmountable obstacle, the audience will view it the same way.
- **State only those negatives that are required and relevant.** Because leaders use negatives to connect with audiences and to spur them to action, they must consciously choose to share only those negatives that will support those goals. Consequently, they choose not to share negatives that are demoralizing or irrelevant, or that cannot be overcome.

No matter how effectively they are stated, the most effective use of negatives is as a springboard into a more positive discussion.

MOVE FROM NEGATIVES TO POSITIVES

While leaders do not shy away from negative realities, they also purposefully move from negatives to positives in their language. In his August 28, 1963, speech in Washington DC, Martin Luther King Jr. capably showed how to make this transition. Midway through his speech, he acknowledged the racism and persecution endured by his audience:[3]

> I am not unmindful that some of you have come here out of great trials and tribulations. Some of you have come fresh from narrow jail cells. And some of you have come from areas where your quest – quest for freedom – left you battered by the storms of persecution and staggered by the winds of police brutality.

By doing so, he legitimized the anger and frustration likely felt by many listening to him. But then he asked his audience to move past it:

> Let us not wallow in the valley of despair, I say to you today, my friends.
> And so, even though we face the difficulties of today and tomorrow,
> I still have a dream. It is a dream deeply rooted in the American dream.

Having made the transition from negatives to positives without dismissing the challenges facing so many in his audience and the country, King was then able to present his vision:

> I have a dream that one day this nation will rise up and live out the true meaning of its creed: "We hold these truths to be self-evident, that all men are created equal."
> I have a dream that one day on the red hills of Georgia, the sons of former slaves and the sons of former slave owners will be able to sit down together at the table of brotherhood.
> I have a dream that one day even the state of Mississippi, a state sweltering with the heat of injustice, sweltering with the heat of oppression, will be transformed into an oasis of freedom and justice.

I have a dream that my four little children will one day live in a nation where they will not be judged by the color of their skin but by the content of their character.

In each stanza, King repeated the parallel structure of a negative to a positive. This reiteration of his dream, the negative that must be left behind and the positive future that would replace it, was a powerful way both to acknowledge the tough realities facing African Americans and the uplifting goals he hoped the Civil Rights struggle could achieve.

While you may not be giving an inspiring talk on civil rights, King's speech demonstrates the ideal way to move from negatives to positives. You can move from negatives to positives using a sentence-to-sentence structure, which can be achieved by introducing a negative as a sentence and then following it with a corresponding positive sentence:

We failed to meet our production targets for the last two quarters. That's why it's critical we address our maintenance issues so we can deliver in the six months ahead.

You can also move from negatives to positives in a single sentence by making the negative the subordinate clause:

While our current rate of spending is unsustainable, this new round of venture financing will give us the time we need to bring our revenues in line with our expenses.

Finally, you can move from negatives to positives by going through all the negatives, and then by making a transition to positives:

Let me begin by acknowledging that the last year has been difficult for all of us. We faced what seemed like a string of crises that have tested us all. There was the merger of our two strongest competitors, which has made it harder for us to win business. There was the unexpected departure of our CEO. And there was the maturation of the cloud computing business, which has put pressures on our margins. These are the challenging realities we face, and I know none of us take them lightly.

Yet, I also know that in spite of these challenges, we grew our revenues and share of market. We created new offerings that will begin to translate to revenue next year. And our retention rate was as high as it has ever been, which is a testament to this executive team's leadership.

These and other positives give me tremendous confidence as we start our next fiscal year. I believe in what we can achieve through the continued focus on the execution of our strategy.

Know That There Is Always a Positive

No matter how dark the situation may seem, know that there is always a positive if you look hard enough. Some years ago I was working with a vice president of an oil and gas company. This executive had to lay off some 30 people in his downstream (retail operations) group. This layoff was not performance based, but was instead driven by the need to reduce costs. The executive was feeling down about the decision, which was not his own. I asked him to tell me what he envisioned saying to his employees.

"Well," he said, "I am going to be straight with them. I will tell them they are getting screwed here and I don't like it."

I played the tape back to my client and asked him how his laid-off staff would feel if they heard him say this.

"Demoralized. Pissed off. Angry at the company."

When I asked him whether that would help at all, he thought for a while and realized that since the decision had been made, there was no reason to make the employees feel worse about it. I asked him what he could say – with integrity – that was positive. He thought for a long time and then said:

Let me tell you this is a decision that has nothing to do with your performance or commitment level, both of which have been outstanding. And I want you to know that you will be getting a generous severance package and my full support as you seek your next job, if you choose to. But I want you to leave with your head held high, and know that you have delivered for this company, and I appreciate your contributions to the organization, but more importantly I appreciate having had the chance to work with you these last few years.

Even in this difficult moment, this leader's ability to find the positives allowed him to provide his employees with a meaningful moment of appreciation and respect. He found a way to deliver the hard news – layoffs and severance packages – in a more constructive way that eased the delivery of the negative message and left the employees feeling appreciated and taken care of.

SUMMARY

Leaders inspire others to make decisions and take actions that lead to lasting change. They inspire their audiences to do so because they lay out a vision for what is possible and can be achieved. They know that negative news has to be delivered along with the positive and find constructive ways to deliver these messages. They know that negatives can be detrimental and make the choice to use positive language not only because it is critical to their success but also because positives allow them to rally others to their cause.

NOTES

1. Roy F. Baumeister, Ellen Bratslavsky, Catrin Finkenauer, and Kathleen D. Vohs, "Bad Is Stronger than Good," *Review of General Psychology*, 5(4) (2001): 323. Available online at file:///C:/Users/User/Downloads/71516.pdf.
2. Daniel Kahneman, *Thinking Fast and Slow* (Toronto: Random House of Canada, 2011), 301.
3. Martin Luther King, Jr, "I Have a Dream," American Rhetoric: Top 100 Speeches, http://www.americanrhetoric.com/speeches/mlkihaveadream.htm. All excerpts are taken from this source.

17

THE LANGUAGE OF LEADERSHIP IS . . . DIRECT

Before the TV show *The Office* debuted on NBC in 2005, the film *Office Space*, released in 1999, offered viewers a chance to laugh and cry at the realities facing many cubicle-dwellers in the corporate world: unfulfilling jobs, ineffective consultants, arbitrary policies, and, of course, terrible bosses.

Peter Gibbons, played by Ron Livingston, is the film's protagonist – a disgruntled programmer at the fictitious company Initech, who is continually frustrated by his ineffective boss, Bill Lumbergh, played brilliantly by Gary Cole. Lumbergh's ineffectiveness expresses itself in many ways: he is officious, has little to no emotional intelligence, and seems to do nothing of value. Yet, the most cringe-inducing Lumbergh moments come when he uses indirect language to ask people to do things.

Early on in the film, Lumbergh walks over to Peter and says, "Hello Peter. What's happening? Um, I'm gonna need you to go ahead and come in tomorrow. So if you could be here around nine that would be great. Oh, oh, yea...I forgot. I'm gonna also need you to come in Sunday, too. We, uh, lost some people this week and we need to sorta catch up. Thanks."

In an act of rebellion, Peter decides not to come in. Lumbergh leaves him a voicemail: "Yeah, hi, it's Bill Lumbergh again. I just wanted to make sure you knew that we, uh, did start at the, uh, usual time this morning. Yeah it isn't a half day or anything like that. So if you could get here as soon as possible, that would be terrific."

It is painful to listen to Bill because he is indirect even as he tries to give directions. Leaders recognize that in all but a few instances, the language of leadership is direct, because directness is crucial to reaching audiences and providing clear thinking that can inspire action.

⌾

YOUR AUDIENCES WANT YOU TO BE DIRECT

To be comfortable with using direct language, you must recognize that your listeners will benefit from — and appreciate — straight talk. As the last chapter suggests, that doesn't mean piling on the negatives. But it does mean presenting a clear, balanced picture. This issue is particularly acute when it comes to giving feedback on performance. Here's Geri Prior, CFO of ICBC, giving me her take on why this indirectness is so common:

> I think it's difficult to be direct in performance reviews. People don't know how to do it tactfully. They worry about hurting people's feelings. They know they have an obligation as a manager, as a leader to provide feedback — they know it's a part of their job. [So even when] they do it...they're not comfortable doing it.

Geri suggests two reasons why providing this feedback is difficult:

> One is they are either not observant, so they can't provide meaning-ful feedback; [the other is that] they do know but they can't have the conversation. So if you assume that you've got competent people in there that are observant...[then why do they] not give direct feedback? Because the conversation is challenging to have in a tactful way.

Geri's correct – many managers and leaders know what they need to say but don't because they can't do so effectively.

It's not just in the business world where indirectness is the norm. Take fundraising. Geoff Lyster, Partner at the global law firm Fasken Martineau Du Moulin LLP and also Chair of the BC Women's Hospital and Health Centre Foundation, explained to me that the key to fundraising is to be direct in asking for support, yet far too many people asking for donations don't come to the point:

> High net worth individuals and organizations that are approached are used to being asked for money all the time. So they are not surprised if you set up a meeting with them. They know what's happening. So if you dance around [asking for money] or kind of half ask, then it reflects on your confidence [in the cause].
>
> So if someone says, "This is what's going on [in our organization], we have this particular need right now [and] I'm hoping that you can help by contributing ____" ... [that's helpful]. It's [more] helpful than just say[ing], "We're doing some really good things, I'm hoping you might be willing to help us in some way," with no clue as to what or how much [they] really want. You need to ask for a specific amount or a range, or present some options.

The kind of indirectness that Geri and Geoff describe is far too typical, and the ramifications can be significant. Here are three examples of the costs of indirectness drawn from my coaching experience:

- A telecommunications vice president who did not tell a subordinate she would not be promoted for fear of "hurting her feelings"; the result was that their relationship gradually became toxic.
- An up-and-coming investment banker who didn't want to alienate his boss by saying he wanted to move to private equity, and so caused shock and anger the day he announced he had secured an internal transfer.
- A partner in a tax firm who would not tell his client what he needed to change (out of fear it would damage the relationship), and was then shocked when the client dropped him for failing to provide value.

These and other scenarios were the result of indirectness. Each individual was well-intentioned. Each sought to "protect" others from harsh realities or difficult feedback. Yet, the result of their efforts was to do both themselves and their audiences a disservice.

But imagine if the speakers I described had been direct; the result in each case would be that they would have the opportunity to influence and inspire their audiences in meaningful ways. For example:

- By telling his subordinate why she was not ready for a promotion, the telecommunications VP could give her a chance to work on her development needs or to pursue a different career.

- By telling his boss he wanted to be in private equity but was willing to give his all while he searched for an opportunity, the investment banker could build an authentic relationship with his boss.

- By telling his clients they had to create a more efficient tax structure, the partner would have kept the relationship strong.

Your audiences want you to be direct with them. I know because they tell us when we conduct focus groups with them about internal communication norms. Here is what Jeff, a middle manager in finance at a forest products company, told us:

> I want my boss to tell me the truth about why I am not being promoted. If I'm meeting my targets and there's another area I need to get better at, tell me. If I'm not able to build my financial modeling skills or be stronger in the room with our divisional executives and leaders, tell me. I need to know exactly what skills I need to improve on because the alternative is that I walk around thinking I'm doing a great job. But no one tells me because they are nice people and they're trying to save me. I don't want to be saved, I want to progress. So be honest with me and tell me.

And here's what Vince, a senior manager in a consulting company, said:

> It's exhausting to have to read the tea leaves all year long because no one ever comes out and says, "You're behind your peers and we're not sure

you'll make partner," or even, "Partner may happen but it's going to be a few more years, so sit tight and do X, Y, and Z to improve your odds." Instead, you have to continually guess based on what projects you are staffed on or who holds the power in the organization. I could spend so much more time on my actual work if people were clear with me.

These quotations typify what we hear from people who are driven, ambitious, and talented – in short, the high-performers that every organization should want to retain and develop. Yet, what they say is not dissimilar from what customers tell us they want to hear from their service providers or from what analysts tell us they want to hear from corporate leadership teams.

BE READY FOR – AND COMFORTABLE WITH – SOME CONFLICT

Another reason many people aren't as direct as they should be is that being direct often results in some form of conflict. The three examples I have provided are also ones where the speakers were trying to protect not only their audiences but also themselves. By using indirect language or by avoiding important conversations entirely, they hoped to avoid having to engage in conflict.

Here's how Liane Davey, Vice President at Knightsbridge Human Capital, a North American leadership development firm, explains it in her 2013 *Harvard Business Review* article, "Conflict Strategies for Nice People":

Do you value friendly relations with your colleagues? Are you proud of being a nice person who would never pick a fight? Unfortunately, you might be just as responsible for group dysfunction as your more combative team members. That's because it's a problem when you shy away from open, healthy conflict about the issues. If you think you're "taking one for the team" by not rocking the boat, you're deluding yourself.

Conflict – presenting a different point of view even when it is uncomfortable – is critical to team effectiveness. Diversity of thinking on a team is the source of innovation and growth. It is also the path to identifying and mitigating risks.[1]

Effective leaders are less concerned to protect their emotional equilibrium, than to inspire others to act. They recognize that direct communication requires the courage to deal with pushback, conflict, and emotional upheaval. And while few leaders enjoy such encounters, the most effective ones see them as a sign of a genuine dialogue that they can use to change thinking.

BE DIRECT, NOT BLUNT

Now, being direct does not mean having a license to say whatever is on your mind. It means making the conscious choice to say exactly what the audience needs to hear from you so their thinking can change and action can follow. Adopting this mindset will allow you to be direct and positive rather than "blunt" or "rough."

I remember coaching one sales executive in a large pharmaceutical company who was extremely proud of his directness. He told me that he never missed an opportunity to give feedback, to provide direction, and to "take my audiences to the Truth Zone."

As part of his initial assessment I interviewed some of his peers and direct reports. They all agreed that he was exceedingly direct – but they all said it was a negative quality. I pressed them for details and they told me that his directness seemed designed to put others down at every opportunity and to bolster his own ego. In a town hall he would respond to a question by stating, "That's an uninformed question and I'm going to tell you why." In another instance, he told a junior sales rep that she was, "not cutting it and just didn't get the strategy." It turned out she didn't understand it because it was needlessly complex, but she was uncomfortable saying that and instead felt shamed.

As I worked with the executive, I saw similar patterns and was able to point out the negative reactions to his directness. He confessed that he was unsure of how to be direct without being hard on people.

My advice to him was to think of the action he wanted to inspire through his directness. If he wanted to inspire people to ask more questions, he should be appreciative of their willingness to ask and to provide them with helpful responses. If he wanted higher performance, he could be direct about not meeting expectations but then have a dialogue around why the strategy wasn't being executed.

In his book *The Hard Thing about Hard Things*, Ben Horowitz writes that you should "be direct, but not mean." He goes on to explain:

> Don't be obtuse. If you think somebody's presentation sucks, don't say, "It's really good, but could use one more pass to tighten up the conclusion." While it may seem harsh, it's much better to say, "I couldn't follow it and I didn't understand your point and here are the reasons why." Watered-down feedback can be worse than no feedback at all because it is deceptive and confusing to the recipient. But don't beat them up or attempt to show your superiority. Doing so will defeat your purpose.[2]

Bluntness is being direct with no consideration of how it will affect the recipient. Leaders, as Horowitz points out, offer direct feedback, but they do so in a way that considers the feelings of their listeners and the goals that they, the leaders, hope to achieve.

AS ALWAYS, BE AUDIENCE-CENTRIC

Remember that what one audience may perceive as direct, another may perceive as rude. Conversely, what one audience may perceive as overly direct, another may perceive as not direct enough. For these reasons, it is important to be conscious of the degree of directness your audience will best respond to.

When I interviewed Dr Greg Wells, Assistant Professor at the University of Toronto and Associate Scientist at SickKids Hospital, he spoke about the need to be direct when working with high-performing athletes:

Direct communication [with athletes] is absolutely crucial. . . . It's funny that the ruthless truth seems to be painful but very effective. I'm a physiologist, I study how the body works. I test people, I give them their test results – and I tell them what their test results mean. . . .

When you're working with elite-level athletes, they're stubborn. They're world class for a reason. They're exceedingly confident. And, sometimes they don't like the results or they don't like the truth, or the truth is painful because it tells them that they have to change.

And so, I've found over the years that sticking ruthlessly to the truth has been difficult but very, very, very, powerful. But it hasn't made me any friends at all!

While high-performing athletes need this kind of intense directness, not everyone is ready for it. So be sure you assess and determine what level of directness is required for your audience to hear you.

Another way you should be audience-centric is by considering the power dynamic between you and your listener(s). One formal expression of power is hierarchy. It is expected that senior people can and should be direct with their subordinates. Executives and managers must set goals, give feedback, and offer guidance on how things should be done. Being very direct is fundamental to the expectations of the role.

Conversely, subordinates speaking to their managers must tread more carefully as their directness is not automatically endorsed by their position within an organization. They must consider the culture of the organization, the receptiveness of their manager, and their own qualifications to bring forward an idea.

Yet, few power dynamics are as cleanly defined as boss/subordinate or subordinate/boss. Far more frequent are peer/peer interactions, or large group settings where multiple parties have varying levels of responsibility and seniority.

The easiest way to assess the hierarchy and consequently the level of directness is first to consider who your real audience is. If you are the VP of product development speaking to your management team, but your real audience is the VP of marketing, you can be direct, since the hierarchy is peer/peer. Alternatively, if you are the controller speaking to the finance leadership team, but your real audience is the CFO, you must tread a bit more carefully, since the relationship is subordinate/boss.

Your CEO may be very open to hearing difficult news while your VP of marketing is anything but – so be sure that you combine your hierarchical assessment with your knowledge of how receptive particular individuals are to directness. By doing so you will be well-equipped to decide what will be viewed as direct and not blunt.

SUMMARY

Well, maybe in summary I could just leave you with a few things you might want to hear. I might get around to telling you or you could just reread this chapter and. . . .

Didn't get it? Let me be more direct.

To lead, you need to convey your thinking with direct language. Your audiences want and need you to be direct, even if their initial reaction is a defensive one. Embrace that conflict as an opportunity to influence and inspire.

NOTES

1. Liane Davey, "Conflict Strategies for Nice People," *Harvard Business Review*, December 25, 2013, https://hbr.org/2013/12/conflict-strategies-for-nice-people/.
2. Ben Horowitz, *The Hard Thing about Hard Things: Building a Business When There Are No Easy Answers* (New York: HarperCollins, 2014), 232.

18

THE LANGUAGE
OF LEADERSHIP
IS . . . CONCISE

et's begin with a story about the power of being concise.

Grace was a vice president of database marketing at a major Canadian bank. Ten years ago her team was using software to do all sorts of brilliant things to improve service to retail customers. For example, if you were a banking customer who got a sudden windfall and deposited a larger-than-usual amount in your account, the software would notice and let a wealth advisor know to place a helpful call. Grace's team was earning recognition internationally in the banking industry, and she was nominated along with two competitors for an innovation award.

The finalists had to travel to London, England, to give a 10-minute presentation that highlighted the innovative way they were using technology to serve customers. I was coaching Grace at the time and was impressed by her non-traditional approach: she would present without a slide-deck.

When Grace arrived she was pleased to find she was going last. The other two finalists stood up and narrated dense presentations that showcased their efforts in great detail. The first one ran out of time without going through his presentation in its entirety. The second started speeding up his rate of word delivery as the time ticked down. He ended on time but nearly passed out from lack of breath.

Then it was Grace's turn. She stood on the stage and paused, looking at each member of the panel. "Ladies and gentlemen, I will be brief – we have harnessed the power of data analytics to allow us to anticipate and meet the needs of our customers. We believe we are the leading bank in the world in how we do this – and I will show you why by sharing three stories with you about customers we delighted."

Nine minutes later she sat down to applause. Shortly thereafter she and her team were awarded the prize.

While her team won kudos for the brilliant work they were doing, the panel took pains to comment on the clarity with which she had presented the team's achievements. Unencumbered by slides, content, and verbiage, she was free to concisely share what proved to be the winning story.

AUDIENCES CRAVE CLARITY – AND BREVITY

Today, readers and listeners want less data and more Grace-type clarity. We are awash in *content*. Our email inboxes overflow with unread messages. Our Twitter feeds refresh every few seconds, disgorging new updates. PowerPoint presentations expand to obese lengths, and individual slides are packed with so much detail that you would need a magnifying glass to read them.

Within most organizations, the meetings we sit in and the people we listen to only add to this feeling of content overload. Typical meetings involve status updates from everyone. Town halls see a parade of executives each presenting detailed results. Even casual interactions are focused on information transfer.

How is this *content* delivered to us? In words. We read, hear, and see more words than ever before. Yet, though we are listening to more *words* than ever before, it can be harder to find powerful ideas within them. Great ideas are drowned out.

✹

LEADERS ARE CONCISE

As a leader, your challenge is having your ideas heard and understood. You can improve your odds by ensuring that your language is concise.

Here's Serge Roussel, Vice President of Finance at Pfizer, on the subject:

> The best leaders, to me, are the ones that…very quickly articulate a message. This will get my attention and I will be in. The best leaders I have seen are the ones that have a very clear message delivered with very few words.

When you want people to listen and take action, being concise is essential. Guy Jarvis, Chief Commercial Officer at Enbridge, echoes Serge's comments:

> Being concise is hugely valuable [for leaders] because people do not have the time to sit around and wait for the whole message anymore.

One of the most interesting perspectives on the importance of using language economically came from Michael Barry, a pro cyclist who rode with Lance Armstrong's U.S. Postal Service Pro Cycling Team between 2002 and 2006, with T-Mobile/HTC Highroad from 2007–2009, and finally with Team Sky from 2010–2012. Michael talked about how important clear and concise communication was to the success of the teams he rode on:

> People, the way that they speak now, there's a lot of filler in their

language.... Being in an international team, we had to be clear and to the point because, otherwise, there's misunderstanding.

So you had to be really clear and to the point. And even like with the radios [used during the races] as well, it's just like, "go," "stop." Like, really just clear, clear communication...just being as clear as possible, we talked about that. Don't say more than five words, it should be to the point: "water," or "I need this," "I need that," "wind coming up." Because as soon as you start dragging it out, then you have room for error, right?

It's the same in the bus....if you're on an all-English-speaking team, it's pretty easy. But if you have two kids in there who speak Italian and they don't speak a word in English...you have to be a lot clearer and use diagrams.

And on [team] Sky, we had a screen and projector. Go through the courses, break it down, this is what you do, you do, you do, you do. Everything was really clear, then we go through it again. You know what your job is today. Yes, I got to do this so everything was reiterated, so it's really always clear. And I think for the most part, when you think about talking about the jargon and communication within the group, it probably is very terse and to the point.

What should you do to keep your language concise and powerful?

THE BEST WAY TO BE CONCISE

The most effective way to be concise when you communicate is not to begin speaking until you have clarity about what you intend to say.

The most common reason people use too many words is that they haven't taken the time to figure out what they intend to say. As a result they force the audience to be "along for the ride" and to listen to far more words than is desirable.

Geri Prior, CFO of ICBC, made this point in our interview:

I think a lot of people, they start thinking when they start writing or when they get up to speak…they don't have their thoughts ordered first, and then it is confusing to listen to them or read their report.

If you are involved in a free-form discussion, catching up with an old friend, or are working through a problem, having too many words won't be a major issue. But if you are in a situation where your intention is to lead and inspire others, this excess verbiage will undermine your ability to motivate others.

A great starting point is settling on the one message you want to deliver (see The Leader's Script® in Chapter 8 for a look at how to produce such a message). Write that message down, or be sure you know it word-for-word.

Then, when you deliver your talk, strip away anything that detracts from communicating that message. In her book *Executive Presence*, Sylvia Ann Hewlett interviews a senior leader who talks about the importance of brevity:

"Executive presence is not necessarily about being formal or abundant in your communication, but rather straightforward and brief," says Kerrie Peraino, head of international HR for American Express. "The more you keep speaking, or explaining yourself, the more you cloud or dilute your core message."[1]

The best leaders not only think and speak with this kind of clarity, they also help others do the same. The result is a focused discussion. Here is how Jeff Medzegian, Director of Supplier Performance at Boeing, does so:

When people come in and give presentations to me…[they] would bring a lot of data and dive in there or we'll get spreadsheets, and we're trying to do reviews of 30 different projects. You don't have time for that. So then I would start helping people by saying, "Before we even get to this . . . tell me what's the one message you want us to get out of this, what is the one thing?" And it was difficult at first, but it really has helped with the efficiency of our reviews.

By asking his team to focus their thinking around a message, Jeff helped them strip away excess verbiage and get to the point.

LEADERS STRIP OUT THE FILLERS

Once you have your message, you will be in a position to assess which words are required to convey it – and to strip away all those that are not. As author Steven Pinker writes:

"Omit needless words . . . ." The trick is figuring out which words are "needless." Often it's easy. Once you set yourself the task of identifying needless words, it's surprising how many you can find. A shocking number of phrases that drop easily from the fingers are bloated with words that encumber the reader without conveying any content.[2]

Pinker's "prime directive" to omit needless words is easier to apply when writing, thanks to the luxury of reading and editing, but is no less relevant to speakers who surround their few pearls of wisdom with an abundance of verbal meaninglessness.

Whether you are speaking or writing, you should follow Pinker's advice and strip away all the "filler" words that attach themselves like barnacles to your more substantive language. Just as barnacles slow the passage of a ship, so too will these filler words slow down your delivery and weaken your message.

There are many categories of filler words; Table 18.1 provides a *concise* list.

So what should you do with this kind of language? Well, um . . . I guess if you are trying to, you know, lead . . . well, at the end of the day it's all about . . .

Table 18.1 Filler Words

"Filler" word category	Examples
Silence Fillers	Um ... Uh ... So yeah ... Right ... You know ...
Unnecessary Add-ons	At the end of the day ... On a go-forward basis ... Just saying ... Net net ... To boil it all down ...
Intensifiers (These become even more egregious when they are applied to absolutes, e.g., *really* unique, *very* perfect; that is, an absolute, which is one of a kind, cannot be modified.)	Really Very Truly Whole Supremely
Useless Adverbs*	Actually Frankly Basically Extremely Definitely Simply
Mincing Modifiers (See Chapter 15 for more about these.)	Just Sort of A bit Perhaps Probably I think I'd guess We might It could
Meaningless Drivel	It's all about ...

*Marcia Riefer Johnston refers to these as "vapid adverbs." She says, "Many adverbs, especially the ones that end with -ly ... have less substance than the weightless, drifting snow that Inuits call weightless, drifting snow." *Word Up! How to Write Powerful Sentences and Paragraphs* (Portland, OR: Northwest Brainstorm Publishing, 2013), 43.

Sorry – got caught up in meaningless drivel.

What you should do is not use any of these fillers. Let your powerful ideas stand on their own merits.

SKIP THE MEANINGLESS PREAMBLES

Finally, you can speak concisely by eliminating the preambles that so often precede substantive remarks. I remember working with Ivan, a project manager at a Calgary, Alberta, electric utility, who was preparing to testify in a regulatory hearing. The utility he worked for had spent years assembling an application to build a new transmission line, and Ivan had been instrumental in choosing the best route.

As we began the mock cross-examination, it became clear that Ivan was smart, dedicated, thorough – but not concise. Here's one line of inquiry:

> **Cross-examiner:** Ivan, can you tell me why route A is the recommended route when it will cut through land where woodland caribou are known to travel through each year?
> **Ivan:** Thank you for that question. I appreciate you asking. You know, there is a lot to consider when selecting routing. On the one hand you have total line distance. On the other hand you have environmental impacts. There is still another hand of cost…but I guess the short answer is that our environmental impact assessment made clear there will be no impact on caribou herds.

When we played back his testimony to him, Ivan acknowledged he was not being concise. He said the reason was he thought that a preamble was important to "show respect" to the questioner and to "set the stage" for his answers.

Leaders know – and Ivan quickly came to see – that such preambles do little more than confuse the audience and waste their time. In a situation like an oral hearing, Ivan was best served giving only the information required by the cross-examiner and no more.

It's not just in oral hearings where speakers could stand to cut the preambles. I often tune out the useless preambles delivered by conference presenters. These individuals often feel the need to "break the ice" before getting to their message. Some of the devices these speakers use include gratuitous flattery:

So great to be back here for the fifth year. The venue is just wonderful. And wow, how about that fruit buffet. Just can't get enough!

Or the non sequitur "icebreaker" story:

Now I know I'm here to talk about what's happening in energy prices these days, but how about those LA Lakers. What is going on with them? And Kobe? No one wants to play with that guy....

Or the overly personal disclosure:

It always scares me coming up here to speak to 500 people. I just pretend you're all naked. That's supposed to work right? Believe me, when they said it would I never believed them, but lo and behold it does. And boy, people, you are HOT!

Such useless preambles are not confined to workplace talks. In fact, the situation where you are most likely to hear a useless preamble is the wedding speech. Such openings are usually cliché-ridden preambles that seem to be pasted in from something out of wedding "mad libs." A typical preamble might go something like this:

Thank you all so much for coming. Many of you have come from far and wide to be here on this very special day. What a lovely service that was earlier, so moving. And how about that bride and groom, don't they both look fantastic? Wow. We couldn't be happier for them....

Spare your audiences. Skip the preamble and get to the point.

Summary

If you want to inspire and move your listeners, be concise. Strip out the verbiage and get to your message. Your listeners will thank you and the applause will come a lot sooner.

Notes

1. Sylvia Ann Hewlett, *Executive Presence: The Missing Link between Merit and Success* (New York: HarperCollins, 2014), 60.
2. Steven Pinker, *The Sense of Style: The Thinking Person's Guide to Writing in the 21st Century* (New York: Viking, 2014), 104.

19

THE LANGUAGE OF LEADERSHIP IS... PROFESSIONAL

It was time for the town hall of a pharma company I'll call RX. The 5,000 employees in attendance were excited about the keynote speaker. Two months ago, their CEO had proudly announced that Khalil was leaving their competitor to take over as RX's head of marketing. This was a real coup; Khalil had earned a reputation as a marketing genius and had helped RX's competitor increase its market share through savvy messaging to physicians who prescribed their drugs.

Now he was on RX's team, and everyone was excited to hear what he had in store. As the town hall began, RX's CEO Rebecca came to the podium and addressed the crowd. Rebecca was known for her polished talks – the organization called her the "Steve Jobs" of pharma. She always came across as supremely precise and professional. Like Jobs, she was known for meticulous preparation, and in her introduction of Khalil it was evident she had invested ample time in positioning him the right way.

After outlining his credentials and qualifications, she wrapped up: "So, in summary, it gives me great pleasure to welcome Khalil to our leadership team. For the last several years we developed a high level of respect for his work when he was working for our competition. We know he is a passionate, driven, genuine person. In fact, we came to admire him so much we decided to hire him. And I believe I speak for us all when I say we are very excited to hear his thoughts on how we can become the leader in our market. Khalil, the floor is yours."

Khalil strode to the podium. He leaned on the podium and took in the applause. "Thank you. Thank you. Now before I get to my presentation...."

The applause continued. The excitement in the crowd was evident. Khalil was clearly feeding off it. He raised a fist, "Yeah, people!"

The cheering continued.

"YEAH!!"

The cheering intensified. Khalil was nearly bouncing in excitement. "F*** YEAH PEOPLE!"

Immediately the cheering stopped. The room went quiet as 5,000 people stopped cheering and looked at each other. Did he really just say that? RX had always been a professional environment where swearing was *verboten*.

Khalil tried to recover, "Uhhhh...OK. Well, now for my presentation."

But it was too late – the shock was so great that the presentation was forever known as the "F-yeah presentation" in the company. And Khalil had dug himself a big hole before his work had even begun.

What had happened? Why had Khalil so misread the audience?

It happened because his desire to be "genuine" and "passionate" overrode his good judgment about what constitutes professional language. The result was that Khalil did damage to his leadership persona and diminished his ability to reach and influence others.

Leaders know that their words must be natural and authentic, but also professional. There is a high standard expected of leaders. We want our leaders to personify professionalism in action and in word. This is why it is crucial that you make your language professional. Here's how you can do this.

KNOW WHAT CONSTITUTES PROFESSIONAL IN YOUR WORKPLACE AND OCCUPATION

The first step in using professional language is to recognize that what constitutes "professional" varies depending on where you work. If you want to lead, you first need to have clarity about what kind of language will reflect professionalism. The variations can be significant between companies.

Chuck Fallon is the CEO of FirstService Residential; he started his career as an investment banker and then held executive roles at a diverse set of companies, including Terminix International (the largest pest control company in the U.S.), Burger King, and Avis. Here he describes three companies with three very different definitions of what constitutes professional language:

> Burger King was very much of a...marketing-driven organization. So [the language] was more narrative and creative and more about leadership and flowery words. It was really driven by the creativity of the agency and how marketing drove that business.
>
> At FirstService, the language is comfortable. It is caring and not necessarily overly sensitive but it is not sharp-elbowed at all. People really care about what you think, and I think they communicate that way.

Then Chuck told me about Avis:

> The language was sharp-elbowed.... "Did you make the number or not? If you didn't, what are you going to do about it? Well you're not getting paid. Alright, come back to me tomorrow. You got a problem with that?" And so yeah, the language was a bit rough. It was a tight ship. And employee engagement was off the charts. So it wasn't a negative environment at all [despite the rough language].

Chuck's experiences illustrate that professionalism varies depending on where you work. An employee at FirstService who went to work at Avis might find the language to be pushy, aggressive, or even rude, while an employee who moved from Avis to FirstService might find the language there to be overly delicate and sensitive.

You need to understand the language of professionalism in the company and industry where you wish to lead and be prepared to adjust accordingly (while staying true to yourself).

BE PROFESSIONAL, NOT CASUAL

You will immediately make your language more professional by avoiding overly casual words and expressions. In her *Harvard Business Review* article, "In Praise of Boundaries: A Conversation with Miss Manners," Diane Coutu asks etiquette writer and syndicated columnist Judith Martin (better known as "Miss Manners") about the lack of etiquette in the workplace. Martin comments:

> Unfortunately, the pseudofriendliness, personal e-mails, and office collections for the umpteenth bridal or baby shower have destroyed the sense of boundaries that characterizes professional behavior. If we hope to reassure our customers that we are indeed professional, we need to be aware of those boundaries.[1]

The need for boundaries extends to your use of language. Select language that positions you as a leader. You can do this by avoiding the following:

- **Too much personal disclosure:** Beware of "oversharing" about yourself in ways that will detract from your leadership presence; no one wants to hear that "this weekend was a real disaster, with my in-laws crashing at our house and driving me and the wife crazy."
- **Overly colloquial expressions:** Instead of saying, "We really killed that deal," say, "We did an excellent job on that deal"; instead of saying, "all us guys and gals" ..., say, "our whole team ...."

- **Unnecessary abbreviations:** Leaders should not say "LOL," "WTF," "OMG," or any other terms that would be more appropriately used by a reality-TV participant.
- **Too-casual personal greetings:** Unless they are running a surf shack or skateboard park, leaders don't refer to people as "man," "dude," "buddy," "honey," "baby," "chief," or any similarly inappropriate terms.

Remember: you are always on stage. While being casual may allow you to connect with your audience, doing so comes at the cost of your leadership presence.

BE PROFESSIONAL, NOT FORMAL

Finally, as you strive to make your language professional, be careful that you do not use words that are overly formal.

When I talk with clients about using professional language, they often reply that to do so would sound too "stiff," "formal," or "uptight." They rebel at the thought of sounding impersonal and creating distance from their listeners. They are right to be concerned about such outcomes, but wrong in associating them with the use of professional language. Instead, they are referring to the dangers of using overly *formal* language.

In the *Merriam–Webster's* dictionary, the adjective *professional* is defined as "relating to a job that requires special education, training, or skill," and, "done or given by a person who works in a particular profession." Conversely, the adjective *formal* means "following or according with established form, custom, or rule."

The difference is important – you want your language to reflect the profession you have chosen. You do not want your language to appear stuffy or snobbish. Just as you select clothing that fits your profession (suit and tie for a banker, safety equipment and steel-toed boots for a mining supervisor), so too should you choose words that fit with your profession and the role you play within it.

Here's Jorina Elbers, Assistant Professor of Neurological Sciences in the division of Child Neurology at Lucile Packard Children's Hospital, Stanford University, sharing her thoughts on professional but not formal language from doctors speaking to patients. Professionalism, she says, is reflected in their:

> ... bedside manner and how [they] interact with patients and their families; the respect that a physician would show the families rather than giving them a diagnosis with the hand on the door knob [as they exit or enter].
>
> That's a really unprofessional way of giving any kind of news. You want to sit down. You want to give eye contact. You want to provide empathy. You want to provide support [and show] engagement through body language. The lack of those things is definitely unprofessional.

As Jorina points out, professionalism does not involve using "medical speak" – it comes from being genuine and warm with an audience who needs a human connection.

If you stay too formal, you'll lose your listeners. Beth had spent five years in private equity as an analyst. She was highly regarded within her firm, which focused on buying debt in distressed manufacturing companies. She exuded confidence and professionalism when she spoke, and was comfortable talking with the firm's partners about "value creation," "exit strategies," "leverage ratios," and "maximizing asset values."

Then Beth was given the CEO role of one of the company's recent acquisitions, a struggling furniture company. She knew her language would come across as too formal, so she resolved to win over her staff by being personable yet professional. She replaced "value creation" with "fixing this business." She replaced "exit strategies" with "getting this business back to health." This put her on a stronger footing with the company and its staff, which allowed her to start working on a recovery plan with them.

BEWARE PROFANITY

A final note on professionalism: beware the swear words. As a leader, you will pay a price for using profanity. Depending on where you work, profanity may be used or even may be the norm. The athletes I interviewed, like Michael Barry who rode for the U.S. Postal team, spoke of "locker room" language that was frequently coarse and profane. Leaders – particularly those who have risen through the ranks – can be easily tempted to bond and fit in by using profanity.

It's not just the world of sports where swearing can be the norm. When I interviewed Rob Gouley, Senior Analyst at OMERS Capital Markets, he was polite, polished and his language was consistently professional, yet, when he enters the trading floor, he explained, the language he and his peers use becomes quite profane:

> [The profanity] has toned down a lot recently. It was much worse 20 years ago before my time. But it's quite common for people to say things there that people would never say outside the trading floor.

When I asked him why, he explained:

> I think it's stress relief. Even the swearing. I think it can be a stressful job because you're constantly dealing with situations that you don't have 100% control over....

Using profanity in environments like the trading floor at the stock exchange may be a quick and easy way of blowing off steam – and of fitting in. But you need to make sure that as a leader you aren't taking an easy path to bonding at the expense of your authenticity. No matter how much it makes you fit in, you will pay a price in the eyes of others for using profanity. It will, at best, maintain your leadership presence by matching the level of discourse, but more likely it will diminish how others see you, as Khalil found out.

This is what happened to Ben Horowitz. In his book *The Hard Thing about Hard Things*, he writes openly about his own relationship with profanity, and the struggles he went through around whether or not to tone down his language after employees continually complained about his swearing:

> After much consideration, I realized that the best technology companies of the day, Intel and Microsoft, were known to be highly profane places, so we'd be off culture with them and the rest of the modern industry if we stopped profanity. Obviously, that didn't mean that we had to encourage it, but prohibiting it seemed both unrealistic and counterproductive.

Horowitz then addressed his employees with his decision:

> We will allow profanity. However, this does not mean that you can use profanity to intimidate, sexually harass people, or do other bad things. In this way, profanity is no different from other language.[2]

Horowitz is to be commended for his self-awareness, willingness to address employee concerns about his use of language, and his strong stance in opposing intimidation and harassment. He is also to be commended for his desire to communicate with authentic, genuine language.

Yet, Horowitz paid a price for his unwillingness to self-censor. Remember: he had embarked upon his self-reflection into the use of profanity *only after employees had been complaining about him!* Listen to what he was told by others:

> "This place is entirely too profane. It's making many of the employees uncomfortable." Others chimed in: "It makes the environment unprofessional. We need to put a stop to it." Although the complaints were abstract, they were clearly directed at me, since I was the biggest abuser of profanity in the company and perhaps in the industry.[3]

Though Horowitz was ultimately very successful professionally, his inability to stop swearing clearly was not an asset in reaching employees and creating a positive culture.

Swearing a lot will never help your cause if your goal is to establish yourself as a leader. Here's Susan Uchida, Vice President of Learning at the Royal Bank of Canada, talking about profane language:

> I think it's never part of the business. I think you never know if somebody is insulted by it. I think it is so drastic, it can suck the air out of a room. You don't know the culture. I saw it here in Toronto. I've seen where people have used – and not even the worst profanity but some profanity and it gets attention and I've seen it in the South [of the United States] where it's actually quite offensive. So you have to be very careful. So I would say that you should never use it.

Are there ever instances where swearing is appropriate? There are some times where you can really show your emotions – but recognize that you may very well pay a price in the eyes of those who are offended.

Remember: you can be authentic and professional *without* being profane.

❧

SUMMARY

Audiences hold leaders to high standards. They expect professionalism from those whom they follow, and that behavior should be reflected in the words leaders use. Know what constitutes appropriate language in your workplace and occupation. Find the middle ground between casual and formal. And skip the swearing.

❧

NOTES

1. Diane Coutu, "In Praise of Boundaries: A Conversation with Miss Manners," *Harvard Business Review*, December 2003, https://hbr.org/2003/12/in-praise-of-boundaries-a-conversation-with-miss-manners/ar/1.
2. Ben Horowitz, *The Hard Thing about Hard Things: Building a Business When There Are No Easy Answers* (New York: HarperCollins, 2014), 144.
3. Ibid., 143.

20

THE LANGUAGE OF LEADERSHIP USES . . . RHETORIC

When we think of the word "rhetoric," what comes to mind? Fancy words? Lofty language? Oratorical eloquence? Some guy in a toga?

Surprisingly, rhetoric is far from fancy-speak. Sure, rhetoric dates back to the ancient Greeks. The Greek philosopher Aristotle (384–322 BC) wrote a famous and highly regarded treatise on the subject that set the stage for everything we have since defined as "rhetoric."[1] But Aristotle wasn't writing about how to speak in bloated, formal, pompous language – his point was, in fact, the opposite. Aristotle's treatise on rhetoric was a document that set forth the art of persuasion.

Rhetoric is, in fact, the single most important handbook ever written on the art of clear, effective communication. For over 2,000 years it has taught readers about the importance of having a single, clear message with a powerful structure. And it has shown us how to use rhetorical devices to bring ideas to life.

You may not know it, but you are probably already using rhetoric. Every time you use a metaphor, "The sun is setting on that industry," or a rhetorical question, "Why are we here? I'll tell you why," or hyperbole, "I am so excited to come to work! I know this project is the most important thing in our lives because of how it will change the world," you are channeling Aristotle and drawing on the power of rhetorical devices. When you fully understand what rhetoric is and how to use it, you will find new ways of bringing your ideas to life and inspiring others to hear and embrace them.

There are many figures of speech or rhetorical patterns that can shape your language. This chapter will explore five of the most common ones. Don't be put off by their names – though alliteration, anaphora, antithesis, hyperbole, and metaphor are all Greek in origin – getting to know them will be well worth your effort and will pay huge dividends when you want to inspire your audience.[2]

MATCH THE SOUND: ALLITERATION

The first and most common figure of speech you can use is alliteration. It is the repetition of the same initial sound in a group of words. You've heard the expression "Build your brand." This use of "b" twice in this short expression is an example of alliteration and it makes the concept more memorable. Why? The "b's" make the two ideas stick together in our minds.

Similarly, when the famed investor Warren Buffett spoke to students at the University of Georgia, he told them that "evaluating a company is within what I call 'my circle of competence.'"[3] The term *circle of competence* is a great use of alliteration, and results in a more memorable idea.

Jamie Dimon, J.P. Morgan Chase Chairman and CEO, uses alliteration in his speech to graduates at Harvard Business School when he tells his audience, "Have many truth tellers around you, not just one."[4] The alliterative expression *truth tellers* – joined by two "t's" – is memorable in a way that another substitute expression would not be. For example, if Dimon had said, "Everyone around you should be honest and not hide the facts from you," that would not have had the same effect nor would it be as memorable.

When you use alliteration, it makes your ideas resonate. Instead of telling your team they have "worked hard, drawn on their talent, and done fabulous work," you could say, "We are a *terrific, tireless, and talented team.*" Same content, more memorable.

REPEAT AFTER ME: ANAPHORA, ANAPHORA, ANAPHORA

This second figure of speech means repeating the same word or words in successive sentences, clauses, or paragraphs. Here's Bill Downe, CEO of BMO Financial Group, using anaphora when speaking to the Greater Milwaukee Committee: "Our customers want to move forward – to buy their first homes, to fund their education, to save for their children's education, or to expand their businesses."[5] This simple use of repetition ("to buy," "to fund," "to save," "to expand") in successive clauses builds dramatic excitement and shows that the CEO's bank is in touch with its customers' needs.

Remember Emma Watson's speech to the UN (discussed in Chapter 14, The Language of Leadership Is...Passionate)? It will come as no surprise that she makes use of rhetoric. Look at how she uses anaphora in the following passage:

I am from Britain, and I think it is right I am paid the same as my male counterparts. I think it is right that I should be able to make decisions about my own body. I think it is right that women be involved on my behalf in the policies and decisions that will affect my life. I think it is right that socially, I am afforded the same respect as men.[6]

The repetition of the phrase "I think it is right" four times in successive sentences builds excitement by connecting all her points, and by doing so, she creates a much more meaningful delivery.

To use anaphora, just think about lining your ideas up and connecting them with the same initial word or phrase. For example, to employees you might say:

I am confident we can beat last year's performance. Why? Because we have a much stronger team. Because we have a far better game plan. Because we have partners and clients who believe in us. And because we have a bigger and more impressive lineup of products than we ever have had.

By repeating words you'll drive home the point for your listeners and help them grasp the ideas you want to emphasize.

It's All in the Contrast: Antithesis

This next rhetorical figure of speech contrasts ideas in balanced phrases or words.

Steve Jobs used antithesis when he said, "Design is not just what it looks like and feels like. Design is how it works."[7] Jobs could have simply said, "Design refers to how a product works," but that would not have been as compelling.

Another example of antithesis comes from Richard Branson in a speech on entrepreneurship, when he said, "You don't need business degrees or vast experience to begin a business; you need a great idea."[8]

The power of antithesis is that you can juxtapose contrasting ideas, and your audience will feel the power of viewing the one idea in relation to the other. If Branson had simply said, "You need a great idea to start a business," it would not have been as compelling as setting that idea against a commonly held view that education and experience are the essential ingredients when building a successful business.

The *contrast* in antithesis gives power to your ideas by creating a dramatic tension. Here's how you can use this figure of speech:

Without: "After last year's setbacks we are ready to step forward."

With: "The last year may have felt like a step back for us all. But we needed to take that step back so that now we can take two steps forward."

And

Without: "After completing the permitting process the time has come to work on our project construction plan."

With: "We just went through five years of hard work to earn the environmental permits for this energy project. Our reward? We can get ready for five more years of challenging, exciting work to build it."

Antithesis transforms serviceable but uninspiring words into memorable language.

JUST TO EXAGGERATE, USE A LITTLE: HYPERBOLE

The fourth figure of speech is hyperbole; this is where you deliberately exaggerate for effect. This is the most incredible, unstoppable rhetorical device. If you use it in your presentations, no audience will ever be anything less than passionately inspired by your brilliance.

See how it works?

In 2012 the writer and artist Neil Gaiman used hyperbole in his commencement address to the University of the Arts in Philadelphia. Urging the graduates to "make good art," he drew on hyperbole to stress they should do so no matter what happened. He told them:

Husband runs off with a politician? Make good art. Leg crushed and then eaten by mutated boa constrictor? Make good art. IRS on your trail? Make good art. Cat exploded? Make good art. Somebody on the Internet thinks what you do is stupid or evil or it's all been done before? Make good art. Probably things will work out somehow, and eventually time will take the sting away, but that doesn't matter. Do what only you do best. Make good art.[9]

Obviously exploding cats and mutated boa constrictors are flights of fancy, but in talking about them Gaiman makes his point – no matter what the world comes to, you should "make good art."

You may not talk about mutating boa constrictors but you can still use hyperbole to help you lead and inspire. For example, let's say you were welcoming new employees to your team. Instead of saying, "You have joined the 174th ranked company on the Fortune 500 and we have an interest in your success and how it will enable us to reach our business goals," you could say:

Welcome to a company like no other. We may be ranked 174 on the Fortune 500 but in my mind we are number one. You could not have joined a better company, and not because of our profits or products ... but because of our culture. We want to make this company the best employer not just in the U.S. but the entire world. And we want to do that by making you more successful than you have ever been.

Over the top? Yes. But that's the point of hyperbole – you exaggerate for effect to show your passion and excitement. It's *so* over the top that people know not to take you literally.

❦

LET ME PAINT A PICTURE FOR YOU:
METAPHOR

Metaphor is our fifth figure of speech: this is when you use an implied comparison between two things that are not normally associated with each other.

Some metaphors are short and sweet. For example, a manager might say to her employee: "Congratulations. Your sales performance has *shattered* my every expectation." She is comparing a sales performance to something else that has the power to shatter an object. A sales performance cannot *literally* shatter something else. But using this metaphor allows the speaker to create a more powerful idea. If this manager had simply said, "Your sales performance was excellent," the idea would have had less of an effect.

Another metaphor commonly used in business is that of a journey. One might say, "We are on a *journey* to make this company the best in our industry." Or, "Our team has traveled a long and winding road that has led to the successful completion of this project."

In a 2013 speech, Ginni Rometty, CEO of IBM, used a metaphor when she talked about the concept of Big Data. She explained:

> Big Data is indeed the next natural resource – promising to do for our era what steam, electricity, and oil did for the Industrial Age.[10]

Rometty's metaphor compares Big Data to other natural resources. This comparison is effective because it suggests the impact Big Data can have on our world and on history. It suggests that Big Data is the driving force for our modern era. But instead of just making that statement, she uses the metaphor because it resonates with all sorts of associations – the power that steam had; the power that electricity had; and implicitly the power that Big Data will have.

Metaphors can be more elaborate and you can draw them out for effect. That's what Jamie Dimon did when he spoke to graduating students at Harvard Business School. He said:

> There's already a book being written on each and every one of you, and people ask you [about] it every single day. If I want to know all about you, all I would need to do is talk to your teachers, your friends, your colleagues, your fellow students, and your parents. I would know if you were trustworthy, hardworking, empathetic, ethical, and if you deliver on your commitments, or if you were lazy and always let people down. It's up to you to determine how you want that book to be written. It's a choice. Don't let others write it for you.[11]

Dimon creates an inspiring idea by suggesting that each student's reputation is being created in the same manner that a book is written. He builds on that idea by telling the students that they should be the authors of their own book. This metaphor of the book helps his audience connect to his way of seeing life – and how you write your own story – far more powerfully than simple advice would.

SUMMARY

These five figures of speech will help you inspire your audience in various ways. Language can be a powerful toolbox for engaging your listeners, and rhetoric is one of your greatest tools for achieving this goal. It can make your ideas more powerful and memorable.

The Greeks may have introduced history to the notion of rhetoric, but business leaders today have abundant opportunities to use these figures of speech. And the more you do so, the more your audience will be moved by your imaginative use of language.

NOTES

1. Aristotle's treatise on rhetoric is variously called *Rhetoric, The Art of Rhetoric,* or *Treatise on Rhetoric.* It dates from the 4th century BC and has defined the rules of persuasion that have endured through time.
2. For a list of the most important figures of speech, including the ranking used in this chapter, see "Top 20 Figures of Speech," Richard Nordquist, About Education, http://grammar.about.com/od/rhetoricstyle/a/20figures.htm; and, by the same author, "Chiasmus (Figure of Speech): Glossary of Grammatical and Rhetorical Terms," About Education, >http://grammar.about.com/od/c/g/chiasmusterm.htm.
3. "Warren Buffett, Speech to the University of Georgia Students, Part I," April 21, 2013, GuruFocus, http://www.gurufocus.com/news/217042/warren-buffett-speech-to-university-of-georgia-students-part-1-archive-2001.
4. "JP Morgan Chase's Jamie Dimon Addresses HBS Students on Class Day," June 4, 2009, Harvard Business School, http://www.hbs.edu/news/releases/Pages/classday2009dimon.aspx.
5. BMO Financial Group, "Remarks by William Downe, Chief Executive Officer, BMO Financial Group at The Greater Milwaukee Committee, Milwaukee, Wisconsin, November 10, 2014," https://www.bmo.com/ci/files/Downe_Milwaukee_Nov1014en.pdf.

6. Emma Watson, "Gender Equality Is Your Issue Too," September 21, 2014, UN Women, http://www.unwomen.org/en/news/stories/2014/9/emma-watson-gender-equality-is-your-issue-too.

7. "Quotations by Author, Steve Jobs (1955–2011)," The Quotations Page, http://www.quotationspage.com./quotes/Steve_Jobs/.

8. Richard Branson, "Opportunity Through Enterprise," Speech Presented at the Commonwealth Day 2013 Observance in Westminster Abbey, http://www.virgin.com/richard-branson/opportunity-through-enterprise.

9. "Neil Gaiman: Keynote Address 2012," Presented at The University of the Arts, May 17, 2012 http://www.uarts.edu/neil-gaiman-keynote-address-2012.

10. Ginni Rometty, "Competitive Advantage in the Era of Smart," Speech to the Council on Foreign Relations, New York City, March 7, 2013, http://www.ibm.com/ibm/ginni/pdf/G_Rometty_Council_of_Foreign_Relations_Remarks_as_prepared.pdf.

11. http://www.syr.edu/news/articles/2010/jamie-dimon-commencement-remarks-05-10.html.

CONCLUSION

In his 2009 book *Free: The Future of a Radical Price*, *Wired* magazine editor Chris Anderson explains how the rise of abundance in the world changes what we value – and what we don't. He notes that, "as commodities become cheaper, value moves elsewhere. There's still a lot of money in commodities ... but the highest profit margins are usually found where gray matter has been added to things."[1]

Anderson cites the music industry as a prime example of this shift. Never before has recorded music been so abundant and so easy to consume. It is easier to acquire it through downloading, easier for musicians to provide it to us, and in all respects it is cheaper than ever before. With this rise of abundance, value has moved to the thriving concert business (I blanch at what I paid recently for tickets to hear U2 play in Toronto). Anderson points out that, "Some bands, such as the Rolling Stones, make more than 90 percent of their money from touring.... And why not? Memorable experiences are the ultimate scarcity."[2]

What do the changing economics of the music industry have to do with becoming an inspiring leader? Simple: the same abundance/scarcity principle applies to both worlds.

Today's business world is awash in communication. Our email inboxes are clogged, our Twitter feeds are ever-refreshing, and our LinkedIn contacts disgorge a daily dose of content. The intensity of most workplaces means more meetings, more conversations, and more interactions than ever before, and more superficial, information-based, jargon-ridden communication.

Yet, in today's business world there is also an increasingly scarce commodity: clear, powerful, inspiring communication. As this information overload increases, so too does our need for *inspiration*. More than ever before we search for leaders who can inspire us to believe and act. We watch TED Talks, follow "thought leaders," and look for those who cut through the background noise, shape our beliefs, and move us to act.

What does this mean for you? Simple: by cutting through the informational jargon and delivering clear, powerful thinking, you will be providing something that is increasingly scarce: inspirational leadership.

CHOOSE TO LEAD, THEN SPEAK AS A LEADER

Let's return to the definition of leadership I put forward in Chapter 1.

A leader is someone who inspires others to act.

Leadership is not based on your title, your education, the number of direct reports you have, or your effervescent personality. Instead, it is based on your ability to define and articulate ideas that others believe in and want to act on.

My view is that if you want to lead in this way, you have to earn the right to be followed. If you want to inspire others, you need to bring forward ideas that others *want* to follow, not ones they *have* to follow. Whether it's top talent who want to work for you, executives who believe your project warrants capital, or peers who choose to commit their heart, soul, and weekends to your initiative, the impact of inspired audiences can be incredible.

If you want to lead, begin by making the choice to view all your communication through the lens of leadership. Look at every interaction as an opportunity to reach others and move them to act. See every meeting, email, presentation, and hallway conversation as a forum to bring forward ideas that inspire others to act. In this day of information overload, you need to stand out by consistently bringing forward clear, powerful ideas with conviction.

Once you start looking at your communication through the lens of leadership, you must say something that is worth listening to. Fundamentally, this means moving from "information to inspiration" – doing the hard work of synthesizing content for your listeners and presenting them with a powerful, focused idea that changes how they think and perhaps how they will act. Nate Silver is an American statistician and writer who became famous for his incredibly accurate predictions of the 2008 and 2012 U.S. Presidential elections. In his book *The Signal and the Noise*, he talks about the scarcity of clarity in an age of information overload: "We're not that much smarter than we used to be, even though we have much more information – and that means the real skill now is learning how to pick out the useful information from all this noise."[3] This skill of being able to glean insight from content – and present it with clarity to the right audiences – increasingly sets leaders apart.

After you have a clear idea, you need to present it the right way. This means getting your "script" right – not a written script *per se*, but rather a focused, intellectual argument that lets your audience know exactly what you believe and why. At the heart of this script is a message – the single, focused idea you want your listeners to walk away with. Having this kind of intellectual clarity before you speak will enable you to be in the moment and to focus on conveying your message effectively to listeners.

Which leads to the final way you can speak as a leader – ensure that when you convey your message you do so with language that energizes and inspires. Nelson Mandela once said, "If you talk to a man in a language he understands, that goes to his head. If you talk to him in his own language, that goes to his heart."[4] Suffice to say, you won't reach anyone's head or heart with confusing jargon; instead, you need to choose words that resonate with your audience, words that convey your vision, your passion, and your confidence in your ideas. You need to choose words that convey your ideas directly, concisely, professionally, and above all, authentically.

IT'S TIME TO LEAD

The psycholinguist Frank Smith once said, "One language sets you in a corridor for life. Two languages open every door along the way."[5]

Whatever your native tongue is, I'd like to leave you with this thought: The words leaders use to share their ideas and inspire others should be considered a separate language, the language of leadership. By choosing to learn this language, to make it your own, and to use it as you share the ideas you believe in, you will open doors not only for yourself but also for those whom you inspire.

I encourage you to lead through language. Whether you want to get approval for a project or change your industry, your audiences will thank you for making the effort to inspire them.

Go forth and lead. I wish you all success in your journey.

NOTES

1. Chris Anderson, *Free: The Future of a Radical Price* (New York: Random House, 2009), 43.
2. Ibid., 127.
3. "'Signal' And 'Noise': Prediction as Art and Science," October 10, 2012, NPR Books, http://www.npr.org/2012/10/10/162594751/signal-and-noise-prediction-as-art-and-science; Nate Silver, *The Signal and the Noise: Why So Many Predictions Fail – But Some Don't* (New York: Penguin, 2012).
4. The Quote Yard, http://www.quoteyard.com/if-you-talk-to-a-man-in-a-language-he-understands-that-goes-to-his-head-if-you-talk-to-him-in-his-language-that-goes-to-his-heart/.
5. John-Erik Jordan, "5 Quotes to Inspire Any Language Learner," Babbel.com, http://www.babbel.com/magazine/language-quotes-01.

ABOUT THE AUTHOR

BART EGNAL, PRESIDENT AND CHIEF EXECUTIVE OFFICER, THE HUMPHREY GROUP INC.

Bart's career has focused on assisting individuals and organizations to develop leadership communication skills. He has spent over a decade working with senior executives and their teams to help them speak as influential, inspirational leaders. His passion is helping individuals and organizations define and communicate ideas that lead to business results.

He began his career with The Humphrey Group in Toronto as a speech writer and coach, and has taken on progressively more senior roles. In 2009 he opened the firm's Vancouver office, in 2011 the firm's Calgary office, and in 2013 oversaw the firm's entry into Mexico. He assumed the CEO role in January 2014 and oversees The Humphrey Group's global growth.

Today, Bart continues to work as an executive coach while designing and leading enterprise-wide programs that foster leadership through communication at all levels. He also works in a communication advisory capacity in areas such as talent management, diversity, investor relations, and on regulated hearings. He writes on leadership communication for leading publications including the *Globe & Mail*, the *Huffington Post*, and *PROFIT* magazine. In 2015 Bart was a receipient of the International Alliance of Women's TIAQ World of Difference 100 Award.

Bart has an Honours BA in history from the University of Toronto. In his spare time he enjoys skiing, road bike racing, and spending time with his wife and son.

INDEX